The African Roscius

The African Roscius

Ira Aldridge

MINT EDITIONS

The African Roscius features work first published between 1847–1849.

This edition published by Mint Editions 2023.

ISBN 9798888970126 | E-ISBN 9798888970270

Published by Mint Editions®

MINT EDITIONS

minteditionbooks.com

Publishing Director: Katie Connolly
Design: Ponderosa Pine Design
Production and Project Management: Micaela Clark
Typesetting: Westchester Publishing Services

*"Mislike me not for my complexion,
The shadowed livery of the burnished Sun."*

—Shakespeare

Contents

THE MEMOIR AND THEATRICAL CAREER
OF IRA ALDRIDGE

To the philosopher, the philanthropist, the physiologist—to the man interested in the whole human family, and capable of drawing liberal conclusions from the various characteristics which, under different aspects, it exhibits, this brief memoir of one who stands forth a conspicuous specimen of a "distinct" and "marked" race, and a living illustration of their intellectual capabilities, will be peculiarly acceptable.

It will tell of an Ethiopian—"a black"—who, notwithstanding the abject state in which most of his kind

"Live, and move, and have their being,"

has obtained, and maintains among us Europeans—"whites"—who deem ourselves to be the most civilized and enlightened people upon God's earth, a reputation whose acquisition demands the highest qualities of the mind and the noblest endowments of the person.

The acquirements of a scholar, the conception of a poet, and the accomplishments of a gentleman, must be united in one individual before he can become eminent as an actor. These mental and physical advantages have been found to exist in an African; and to such a degree are they by him exhibited, that he, in his single person, and as a champion of his sable brethren, gives the lie direct to the most "refined" among us who, in his prejudice, his exclusiveness, and his ignorance, shall harbour the remotest doubt of an African being, to all intents and purposes,

"A man and a brother."

It is not, however, the present endeavour of the writer to "point a moral and adorn a tale"; but to give, in the fewest possible words, a concise history of one whose career, describe it as you may, cannot fail to fill the reflective mind with thoughts of deepest interest. It is impossible to regard one man of colour as a being of extraordinary faculties, possessing a soul capable of appreciating, and endowments equal to the representation of immortal Shakespeare's great creations, and not sigh in serious contemplation of the wrongs of thousands of his countrymen, treated by their paler brethren as mindless, heartless, soulless, feelingless clay, bearing the corporeal impress of humanity, but cruelly or thoughtlessly denied its spiritual attributes. No—a moral lesson *will* present, and even intrude itself with the simple fact, that the swarthy native of Africa is as capable of cultivation as the fairest son of

Albion: a fact in which the better portion of mankind rejoice, and one from which the advocate of slavery turns, but turns in vain, for Truth must in time prevail.

Mr. Ira Aldridge, the gentleman whose memoir is here given, has been long celebrated in the provinces, and not altogether unknown in London, as a performer of surpassing excellence. His fame as an actor has extended far and wide throughout Great Britain, but not until now has the Metropolis become perfectly acquainted with his singular merits. His recent appearance at the Surrey Theatre has created not only a sensation in the theatrical world, but a degree of curiosity throughout society in general; and the novelty of his performances, and his unequivocal success, arc matters so striking and suggestive, that a brief account of his origin and professional progress, requires no apologetic preface; and we verily believe that the Anti-Slavery Society have not published a tract containing more incontrovertible evidence of the African's natural claims, than may be found in these pages.

Well-informed people need not be told that a great amount of the highest order of human intelligence is to be met with in people of colour. We have Africans who have attained eminence in the arts and sciences. In the Church, the Law, and in Medicine—in all our professions and trades, have they won honours and wealth; and the hue of the skin is known to be no natural impediment to the acquirement of learning, the cultivation of ingenuity, and the practice of virtue; but Mr. Aldridge is, we believe, the first born negro who has earned for himself a reputation in the highest walks of the Drama, and lie deserves all the credit of having so signalized himself.

We cannot pay to the inky-visaged children of the Sun those personal compliments which are often lavished upon fairer faces. There is black marble as well as white; but those varied tints which captivate the eye—the beauties of colour—that are not even "skin deep," and such as the rose, the lily, the violet, and other flowers display, are peculiar to European countenances. The "pure red and white," however, even in contrast to the blackness with which the Devil is painted, what are they in reality to the scientific and philosophic observer?—What are they in the eye of our common Creator? With such disadvantages as strongest prejudice can create, and generous natures cannot entirely overcome, it is no small triumph to Mr. Aldridge that the following lines have been addressed to him by one of our countrywomen who, in a spirit liberal and commendable, has availed herself of language which, we think, no impartial witness of the African's performances can say is misapplied;—

> *"Thine is the spell o'er hearts*
> *Which only Acting leads;*
> *The youngest of the Sister Arts,*
> *There all their beauty blends:*
> *For ill can Poetry express*
> *Full many a tone of thought sublime*
> *And Painting, mute and motionless,*
> *Steals but a glance of time.*
> *But by the mighty Actor brought,*
> *Illusion's perfect triumph's come:*
> *Verse ceases to be airy thought*
> *And Sculpture to be dumb."*

Ridicule, that powerful weapon even in the hands of fools, assails those who wear

> "The shadowed livery of the burnished Sun,"

more than all the other sons of man upon the face of the globe. It is only in their vilest degradation and deepest misery—it is only in picturing Blacks torn from their homes and dying by dozens in the fœtid hold of a ship, or suffering the crudest tortures of slavery, that the generality of people cease to laugh at them. Their very virtues are turned against them in the shape of distorted or exaggerated facts, and from a long-established custom it has become almost a fashion to indulge in lampoons against the sable fraternity, to exult in caricatures of negro peculiarities. But they are destined to outlive every prejudice. The author of the latest burlesque of the day says, in "The Golden Branch," and in reference to the once-popular, but foolishly-worded ballad of "Cherry Ripe,"

> *"Must it yield the prize of song*
> *To 'Lucy Neal' and 'Lucy Long'?"*

That it has done so is very certain, for "The Ethiopian Serenaders" have lately created among us quite a rage for such productions as the latter; and their performance of negro melodies and pourtrayal of negro character have delighted, day after day, and night after night, without intermission, crowded audiences, principally consisting of the nobility and gentry of this country.

"It takes a clever man to make a clown"; and the acuteness, humour, drollery, and downright absurdity of the negro are all evidences of his superior capabilities, the more striking when we compare them with the stolid natures of our own peasantry, and that "gentle dulness" to be found among others whose lack of brilliancy is not because no pains have been bestowed upon them in the way of polishing—people whose opaque qualities are eclipsed by the native lustre of the "black diamond."

As the foulest waters in time purify themselves, and, in their natural transparency show that which polluted them collected at the bottom, so shall we in time see the character of the man of colour divested of the ignorance, the absurdity, and the humiliation with which it is associated. His simplicity, his fidelity, shrewdness, conscientiousness, gratitude, and even his piety, have never been questioned. These "harmless qualities" of the head and heart have been allowed him, while higher attributes—if higher there be—have been denied, and his aspirations have been the constant theme of broad satire and vulgar personality. Man is the creature of imitation; but an African's emulation, according to the notions of many, must be limited to the prejudice, caprice, and fastidiousness of white men. Such barriers, however, give way, when Education, with indiscriminate hand, comes to the help of the most despised, and brings them to their proper level:—

"For 'tis the mind that makes the body rich."

And yet amid all our moral, social, and religious improvements, how many of us may be shamed by the untutored child of nature—the wildest savage of the uncultivated wilderness! More rude, however, than we have been no Hottentot can ever be; but in the most primitive specimens of the latter tribe are to be found attributes that adorn humanity, and few in comparison that disgrace it. Some of our sweetest and most plaintive melodies take their origin from the original compositions of the Blacks, especially those of the West India plantations, where no labour is performed without a vocal accompaniment. The writer of these lines has heard them join in choruses of rude, but perfect harmony, to verses, constructed for the occasion just as the leader's mind may be prompted by external objects, but never without some rhyme and reason, and a strong dash of poetic fancy.

No man can be more in earnest at one time and more in joke at another than the regular Coast of Guinea negro: the very essentials of genius. The Red Indian has no fun in him; the like may be said of many a narrow-minded man of business, who has no soul for anything approaching the ridiculous—aye, or the sublime either; and, consequently, but little soul at all. The Indian's character, however, wild as it is, is trained to seriousness and self-command. Not so the Negro. He is more a child of nature than the sojourner in the solitary woods: more so than the Hindoo or any of the East Indian tribe; and, unfortunately, less respected, because less dangerous; but he is more to be depended upon, and more tractable, than any other uncultivated being. Thus are his good and amiable qualities taken advantage of by his cruelest enemies, among whom we may reckon a considerable portion of a country—the United States—which boasts of its love of freedom, and bawls aloud its desire to cultivate universal fraternity, liberty, and equality!

Thus premising, in order that the reader may attach some importance to the subject before him, we commence the history of the AFRICAN ROSCIUS, as Mr. Aldridge has been styled from his early assumption of the sock and buskin. We must first, however, refer to his progenitors. His forefathers were princes of the Fulah tribe, whose dominions were Senegal, on the banks of the river of that name, on the west coast of Africa, to which shore one of our early missionaries found his way, taking charge of the father of Mr. Aldridge, in order to qualify him for the work of civilising his countrymen. From what we can gather, his grandfather was more enlightened than his subjects, probably through the instruction of the missionary, and proposed that his prisoners taken in battle should be exchanged, and not, as was the custom, sold for slaves. This wish interfered with the notions and perquisites of his tribe, especially his principal chiefs, and a civil war raged among the people. During these differences, the father of Mr. Aldridge, then a promising youth, was taken to America by the missionary, and sent to Schenectady College, near New York, to receive the advantages of a Christian education. Three days after his departure, the revolutionary storm which was brewing, broke out openly, and the advocate of humanity, the reforming Prince, was, together with his whole family, and personal attendants and connexions, savagely butchered; the missionary escaping with his young charge just in time to avoid a similar fate.

Mr. Aldridge's father remained in America until the death of the rebellious chief who had headed the conspiracy, and reigned instead of the murdered prince. During the interval he had become a minister of the gospel, and was regarded by all classes as a man of uncommon abilities. He was, however, desirous to establish himself at the head of his tribe, possess himself of his birthright, and advance the cause of Christianity among his countrymen. For this purpose he returned to his native country, taking with him a young wife, one of his own colour, whom he had but just married in America. To this step he was prompted by the advice of his white friends, who, doubtless, looked forward to his reign as one calculated to encourage the growth of those "Gospel seeds" which religious zeal had planted among the children of the Fulah tribe. Their pious hopes and intentions were frustrated. Mr. Aldridge, sen., no sooner appeared among the people of his slaughtered father, than old disagreements revived, and two opposition parties were formed. Civil war again broke out, and in the struggle of contending chiefs, the enlightened African Was defeated, barely escaping from the scene of strife with his life, and for sometime unable to quit the country, which was watched by numerous enemies anxious for his capture.

During the first month of the arrival of Mr. Aldridge's parents, he, the subject of this memoir, was born; but nine years elapsed before the proscribed family escaped to America. All this time they were concealed in the neighbourhood of his foes, enduring vicissitudes and hardships that can well be imagined, but need not be described. As is always the case under such circumstances, for all men, more or less, depend upon one another, there was a faithful adherent, whose services mainly helped to save the lives of the rejected prince, and his wife and son. He accompanied those whom he so served to America, and there Mr. Aldridge, sen., returned to his ministerial duties, influencing aright the minds of people of his own complexion, in that country instead of his own.

The present Mr. Aldridge recollects that when a child, some eight years old, playing at the door of a hut where he resided, some warriors belonging to his father's enemies were passing that way, and noticed his resemblance to their fugitive chief who was then, unknown to them, in the neighbourhood. Upon their making inquiries about the boy, the woman of the hut, without betraying alarm, claimed him as her daughter's child, and he was unmolested. A narrow escape for the future African Roscius. Thus was he saved in his infancy to vindicate in his manhood the cause of his whole race; thus was he snatched from after participation in, or falling a victim to, the tragedies of real life practised by his countrymen, that he may among more civilized people, and before applauding numbers, revel in mimic strife! The Negro-boy of Senegal, whose life was so in jeopardy, had a strange career before him!

There may be something suggestive of ridicule in the thought of a black preacher, and Heaven knows there have been enough burlesques written and drawn to associate the idea with preposterously absurd notions of "nigger" eloquence and theology; be that as it may, it should be remembered that sterling merit ought to be measured by the means possessed for working good, rather than by the amount obtained, and Mr. Aldridge's father did not live in vain. Here is a notice of his death, as it appeared in the public papers so late as 1840:—

At New York, on the 27th of September, the Rev. Daniel Alridge, father of Mr. Ira F. Alridge, the celebrated African Roscius. There are few individuals who have been more generally useful than the Rev. Mr. Aldridge, and whose loss will be more severely felt in New York among his coloured brethren, to whom he was endeared by his faithful

We now come more immediately to the career of the African Roscius. His mother died in 1818, leaving but two surviving children, out of a numerous family. One of these, Mr. Aldridge's remaining brother, was murdered at New Orleans some few years ago. He incurred the anger of some whites, in a gambling house, and, during a quarrel, one of the "free and enlightened citizens" gave him his *quietus* with a bowie knife. Being a "nigger," of course no inquiries into the transaction were made, and no inquest was held upon the body.

Mr. Ira Aldridge was intended by his father for the Church. Many a white parent has "chalked out" in vain for his son a similar calling, and the best intentions have been thwarted by an early predilection quite in an opposite direction.

In sober seriousness we can well account for the father's choice, one so in keeping with his own aspirations; and we can easily imagine his disappointment upon abandoning all hope of seeing one of his blood and colour rivalling in reason and rhetoric the most favoured servants in the service of his great Master.

The son, however, began betimes to show his early preference and ultimate passion. At school he was awarded prizes for declamation, in which he excelled; and there his curiosity was excited by what he heard of theatrical representations—representations, he was told, which embodied all the fine ideas shadowed forth in the language he read and committed to memory. It became the wish of his heart to witness one of these performances, and that wish he soon contrived to gratify.

His first visit to a theatre fixed the great purpose of his life, and established the sole end and aim of his existence. He would be an actor. He says at this hour that he was bewildered, amazed, dazzled, fascinated, by what to him was splendour beyond all that his mind had imagined, and mimic life so captivating, that his own real existence would be worthless unless he in some way participated in such imitations as he witnessed. An actor lives to pourtray other's feelings, not his own; Hamlet describes him.

To those who have not visited the United States, the full extent of young Aldridge's presumption cannot be easily comprehended. In that "Land of Liberty" the coloured portion of the population are denied all opportunity of advancement in common with their more fortunate, because paler, brethren. To be of African origin, is to be a "nigger," a conventional term of reproach and contempt; and "niggers," in America, are excluded those places of public entertainment and public worship wherein "pale faces" assemble.

In one theatre only (the Park) an obscure portion of a highest gallery is set apart for people of colour, and there they may be seen, a dark mass of shining ebony faces, relieved by the ivory teeth shown upon every slight incitement to risibility. Here the most respectable are expected to herd with sweeps and pickpockets. No other places must they occupy. So young Aldridge was cut off from witnessing the best performances, and in common with many of his colour, felt severely the distinction which unjustly marked the difference which God's hand had made, and no mortal endeavour could remove.

The sons of "the star-spangled banner" which "Liberty upreared," designedly conspire to humiliate and keep in degradation the race over whom that banner waves in vain, as though they feel convinced that the only difference between the Yankees and their slaves, lies in their relative social positions, and to allow the blacks the chance of improving their condition, would be the sure means of raising them in every respect to a level with the whites. It is, on the other hand, but natural in man to hate those whom they injure—hence we may account for the contumely invariably thrown upon a person of colour by a veritable Yankee. But there is nothing that the enthusiast will not attempt. Difficulties but "spur the sides of his intent," and despite his one personal disadvantage, and, among other numerous and serious impediments, and with a slight hesitation in his speech, Mr. Aldridge became a candidate for histrionic fame.

"Go ahead" is the word in America, where people act more than they think. Our stage-struck hero was not singular as to progression. He fell to work, and studied the part of Rolla, in the play of *Pizarro*, and in that character he made his "first appearance on any stage." This was at a private theatre, where he was singularly successful, and all his fellow-performers were of his own complexion; and, to use his own words, "the gentle Cora was *very* black, requiring no small quantity of whiting, yellow ochre, and vermillion to bring her cheek to the hues of roses and lilies,"— such a face as Sheridan describes in the text. There are many among us who would gladly witness the endeavours of such a company.

Shakespeare decidedly never wrote for such a *troupe*, but he deigned to draw the Moor, Othello, one of his choicest creations, and in pourtraying the immortal part of man he described what was universal. But fancy a black Juliet! And why not? May there not be an Ethiopian Juliet to an Ethiopian Romeo? So reasoned and so *felt* the coloured members of the amateur corps, when Mr. Aldridge undertook to perform the lovesick swain in a sable countenance. Certain Yankees, with a degree of illiberality peculiar to *some* "Liberals," had no notion of such indulgences being allowed to "niggers," whose "tarnation conceit and *considerable effrontery* licked nature slick outright." One Stephen Price, a manager of some repute, became actually *jealous* of the success of the "real Ethiopians," and emissaries were employed to put them down. They attracted considerable notice; and people who went to ridicule, remained to admire, albeit there must have been ample scope for the suggestion of the ridiculous. Riots ensued, and destruction fell upon the little theatre. Of course there was no protection or redress to be obtained from the magistracy (for, unhappily, they were whites), and the company dissolved, much to the chagrin of the Juliet elect, who declared that *nothing but envy* prevented the blacks from putting the whites completely out of countenance.

It was about this time that the celebrated and inimitable mimic and comedian, Mr. Mathews, was on a tour through the United States, from which he brought materials for making many a night "At Home," before an Adelphi audience. He chanced to see Mr. Aldridge on the stage, and made the most of what he saw. The African Roscius thus, at a public dinner in this country, gave his version of the story:—

"Mr. Mathews paid a visit to the theatre on one of the evenings of my performance, and this occurrence he has made the vehicle for one of the most amusing anecdotes in his well-known 'Trip to America.' There is certainly a good deal more in the manner of his telling the story, than in the matter, and he has embellished the whole circumstance with a great many fictitious variations, not the less amusing because untrue, but which are pardonable enough in such a work as Mr. Matthews's, the materials of which are acknowledged to have been made up as much of fiction as of truth. He says that on the occasion alluded to I played Hamlet, and in the celebrated soliloquy, 'To be, or not to be,' on my coming to the passage 'and by opposing end them,' the similarity of the sound of the words reminding the audience of the negro melody of 'Oppossum up a gum tree,' they loudly called for it, and the polite request Mr. Mathews makes me accede to in the following elegant language:—'Well den, ladies and gemmen, you like Oppossum up a gum tree better den you like Hamlet? Me sing him to you'; which I, according to the anecdote, did three or four times, much to the exquisite edification of my black hearers, and then resumed my part of the pensive prince. The truth, however, is, that I never attempted the character of Hamlet in my life, and I need not say that the whole of the ludicrous scone so well and so humorously described by Mr. Mathews, never occurred at all."

Mr. Aldridge was bent upon witnessing the performances which took place in the country of his father's adoption, and opportunities for so doing presented themselves under the following, to him fortuitous, circumstances:—

He had a schoolfellow who was in the habit of taking Mr. Henry Wallack's dresses to the Chatham Theatre, and the acquaintance of this boy he assiduously cultivated. With a little contrivance and the assistance of this privileged individual, young Aldridge obtained an introduction to the mysteries of the Stage. The boy soon after died of the yellow fever, and the coloured aspirant eagerly tendered his services, and obtained the wished-for *entree* to "behind the scenes," by becoming the bearer of the leading actor's dresses, and making himself generally useful in the way of running to and fro. This employment, if known to his father, was not that in which he wished to see his son engaged; but amply was that son repaid for his services, by being permitted to gaze upon the scenes which presented themselves.

It has been said by good-natured people who rejoice in distorting facts to the prejudice of those to whom they can be disadvantageously applied, that Mr. Aldridge, when a youth, was the errand-boy of Mr. H. Wallack, and in that capacity picked up whatever theatrical knowledge he acquired. There is no doubt but he availed himself as much as possible of whatever lessons fell in his way, and the greatest actor of any age must have done something of the kind; with this difference, that others had less difficulty in obtaining instruction. Young Aldridge derived no pecuniary profit from his services, but was too happy to render them in exchange for the delight he experienced in gaining admission to the precincts of what he most admired. There the young Roscius hung about the "wings," receiving intoxicating pleasure, listening with rapture to the wildest rant, and strengthening his hopes of emulating the most admired actors who presented themselves. But a sudden termination was put to his nightly enjoyment; through the interest of Bishops Brenton and Milner, he was entered at Schenectady College, near New York, in order to prepare himself for the ministry; and here for a while he entered into theological studies. Notwithstanding the progress he made in learning, he lacked advancement in his religious profession. No qualities of the mind could compensate in the eyes of Americans for the dark hue of his skin; the prevailing prejudice, so strong among all classes, was against him, and it was deemed advisable to send him to Great Britain. He was accordingly shipped for the Old Country, and entered at the Glasgow University, where, under Professor Sandford, he obtained several premiums and the medal for Latin composition.

Here he remained about eighteen months, when he broke entirely from the scholastic thraldom imposed upon him.

Even religious pursuits could not damp his ardour for the Stage. His early preference "grew with his growth and strengthened with his strength"; and while yet young he started for England, determined to make an attempt to appear in public before an audience who, whatever the severity of their criticism, he believed, would not condemn him on account of colour.

It was in the year 1825 the African Roscius came to England—the Old Mother Country whom he had so often heard reviled in the New World, but to which, in common with every American (whatever they may affect to the contrary), he looked with respect and deeply-rooted interest: feelings more or less disguised and suppressed among the free and enlightened Yankees, as men are wont to hide what does not agree with their vanity. He brought with him no transatlantic recommendations. An actor of colour was a novelty in this country not tolerated in that. Here we have distinctions without differences—there they have no distinctions but differences that are exceedingly great. "Without a friend," we are told, "the world is but a wilderness." There is much truth in the saying, for whatever our station, we are never wholly independent of one another in a social community. A man, nevertheless, may be his own friend to a very great extent, and Mr. Aldridge found that he had few others than himself to rely upon. He brought with him, however, a letter of introduction from Mr. Henry Wallack, whose knowledge of him and his character has been already alluded to. He had now to hammer his way into the theatrical world, and sought an opening for applying "the wedge." A very small aperture presented itself, but that was enough, for, as in rending timber, all depends upon the power and skill that are applied to the opening; and public opinion, however hard and stubborn, seldom fails to yield to the force of merit, provided it be properly and perseveringly brought into action.

Mr. Aldridge commenced at the Royalty, at the East End, under the management of Mr. Dunn, where he first felt the British pulse, and found it favourable to his pretensions. This was in 1826, soon after his arrival from Glasgow.

He made his *debut* as *Othello*, in which he was highly successful. Thus encouraged and strengthened he procured an engagement at the Cobourg, where Messrs. Leclerc, Davidge, Hornblower, and Beugough, were the managers; here he played Oroonoko, Gambia, Zarambo, and or two characters, and obtained great applause.

While there, he entered into an engagement—a solemn one, which, when once made, is peculiarly and particularly binding on both sides—he entered "the holy bonds of matrimony," and undertook to perform the part of a good husband for the rest of his life, to an English lady of respectability and superior accomplishments. The manner in which the match came about has a dash of romance in it, and may be thus briefly told.

Mr. Aldridge, after performing Gambia, in *The Slave*, was invited by a friend to visit a private box, to receive the congratulations of a party who had witnessed his acting, and, from the interest he had excited in their minds, had expressed a desire to see the hero of the play in *propria persona*. The actor was formally introduced, and in that short interview commenced an intimacy which, six weeks after, ended in his marriage with a lady who was present, the natural daughter of a member of Parliament, and a man of high standing in the county of Berks. The lady played, to some extent, a modern Desdemona to Mr. Aldridge's Othello, for he unexpectedly had the power to say, in reply to relations—

> *That I have ta'en away this old man's daughter,*
> *It is most true; true I have married her.*

He was not accused of using "drugs, charms, conjuration, or mighty magic," in obtaining the lady whose affections came to him—

> ———*By request and such fair question*
> *And soul to soul affordeth.*

But her father was much after Brabantio's way of thinking. His eyes mental and physical were not like those of the Duke, who said:—

> *If virtue no delighted beauty lack,*
> *Your son-in-law is far more fair than black.*

Mrs. Aldridge "saw her husband's visage in his mind," and that, we can venture to say, if it has changed at all, has improved by time and trial. Ever since her marriage she has accompanied her husband upon his professional journeys, and his theatrical campaign has been a long one, for there is no British town containing a respectable theatre which has not been crowded to witness his mimic art.

Thence Mr. Aldridge went to Sadlers' Wells, where he performed for a few nights in several leading parts; and next to the Olympic. Thus he modestly and hesitatingly, as it were, edged himself in, tremblingly alive to the prejudice with which he had previously had to contend—a prejudice to which, indeed, he had from infancy been taught to *submit*, however keenly he felt its influence and however plainly he saw its cruel injustice. But he was young; and a genial soil and atmosphere soon causes a sapling tree to take root and spread forth its branches. He had found the true Land of Liberty, and he saw a fair prospect of prospering in it. Having, one may say, felt his way thus far in comparative obscurity, he withdrew into the provinces, the better to fit himself for a greater trial in the metropolis. He accordingly took a country tour, acting in succession at Brighton, Chichester, Leicester, Liverpool, Manchester, Glasgow, Edinburgh, Exeter, Belfast, and so on, returning to London after a lapse of seven years, an apprenticeship which he had turned to good account. During this time Mr. Aldridge had studied deeply and laboured hard at his profession. In every provincial town that he had visited his reception had been flattering in the extreme; and his fame as a country actor, as is generally the case in such instances, had reached the capital.

Notwithstanding the favourable impression "The African Kean," as he was then termed, made wherever he appeared, he repeatedly failed in procuring an engagement at Dublin. Mr. Calcraft, the spirited and accomplished manager of the Theatre Royal, could not be prevailed upon by letter to accept the services of the man of colour, at a venture: there was "something so absurd about it." Mr. Aldridge, therefore, went there at his own cost, and had an interview with the manager. The result was favourable to his ambition, and he was engaged "for a limited number of nights," as the saying goes, establishing a popularity which has never since abated.

Edmund Kean had been previously secured to appear at this theatre; and the management endeavoured to disuade Mr. Aldridge from taking the part of Othello, as the celebrated tragedian was known to complain if his favourite characters were played just previously to his acting them himself. Mr. Aldridge was urged to come forward as Zanga, but he persisted in playing Othello, and had his way. He performed as Othello in December, 1831, and made a great hit. The Dublin people were surprised and delighted. His "sable suit" gave him additional interest in the eyes of the warm-hearted Hibernians, and the newspapers spoke in glowing terms of his rare abilities. This was the first hold that he took upon the British public, because his first appearance before an important tribunal belonging to it. He subsequently ran through his list of favourite characters, viz.: Zanga, Rolla, Gambia, Alhambra, Mungo, etc., in all of which he gained enthusiastic applause. From the many favourable critiques which appeared at the time, we will only quote the following, which by no means contains the greatest amount of praise:—

Mr. Aldridge's first appearance was in a character in every respect suited to his genius, and most strongly calculated to draw forth those extraordinary powers, of which this actor is so distinguished a master. In all those parts where Desdemona calls into action on the part of the noble-minded Moor the softer and finer feelings of the heart, as, for instance, when she pleads for the restoration of Cassio, his responses were delivered in a manner so chaste, tender, and affectionate, that they were deeply felt by the whole audience. Many of those passages expressive of the finer feelings of our nature were most beautifully delivered in a softly subdued tone of voice, which was remarkable for its clearness and distinctness of tone. It was not, however, until Iago had roused his mind to jealousy that the actor became truly terrible and sublime. Beautifully and appropriately as were the softer feelings displayed and expressed, it was in the expression of the strong passions of jealousy and revenge that were raging in the bosom of the distracted Moor that Mr. Aldridge rose to a degree of excellence that we have never seen surpassed, albeit that we have seen the first of his contemporaries in the same character. When Iago began to pour his domestic poison into the ears of Othello, and he became alternately jealous of Desdemona's virtue and doubtful of Iago's honesty, his bursts of feeling, succeeded by fierce ebullitions of passion, were at once masterly, grand, and peculiar; and when in the agony of his soul, lie gave vent to the passage,

"Who doats, yet doubts;
Suspects, yet strongly loves,"

there was not one solitary individual amongst the audience whose heart did not feel, and whose hands did not applaud to the very echo, the soul-stirring eloquence with which the passage was delivered, whilst the dark and broad features of the actor presented to all who beheld them a faithful index of the contending passions which had placed his soul upon the rack. His seizure of Iago, when he seeks to extort from him some proof of Desdemona's dishonesty was also quite original, and well executed. Indeed, his entire representation of Othello is a masterly performance, as cleverly executed as it is originally conceived, and one which will never fail to convince any intelligent audience that the actor possesses a genius not unworthy of the fame he has acquired.

Edmund Kean came to Dublin while the African was there and saw him act, upon which, with the good nature conspicuous in all he did, he gave him a letter of recommendation to the manager of the Bath Theatre, to the following effect:—

Dublin, January 3, 1832

Dear Bellamy,

I beg to introduce to your notice Mr. Aldridge, the African Roscius, whose performances I have witnessed with great pleasure. He possesses wondrous versatility, and I am sure, under your judicious generalship, will prove a card in Bath. I have not yet recovered from the fatigues of my journey, but hope to be myself in a day or two.

I remain, dear Bellamy, truly yours,

E. Kean

Upon referring to the playbills of the day, we find that which was issued for Mr. Aldridge's benefit, on Wednesday, December 21, 1831, contains this heading:—

"The African Roscius having been received by the Dublin Audience on each evening of his performance with enthusiastic applause, will ever feel most grateful for the honour conferred upon him, and considers the approbation of the Irish Public as one of the proudest and most distinguished testimonies which has ever been bestowed upon his professional exertions."

Upon this occasion he performed Gambia, in *The Slave*, and Mungo, in *The Padlock*; and, in the latter character, he introduced, "by particular desire," the comic nigger song of "Oppossum up a Gum-tree."

At Bath Mr. Aldridge was, if possible, more successful than in Dublin. It is, however, unnecessary to follow his every footstep from town to town during his continued successes. At Belfast Charles Kean played Iago to his *Othello*, and he Aboan to Charles Kean's *Oroonoko*.

Sheridan Knowles was among those who at that period complimented and encouraged the "only actor of colour upon the Stage." And the testimonials and letters of congratulation and approval which he then received would fill a book, while provincial criticism was uniformly in his favour. We may here extract from a paper a specimen of the general tone of reviews which his acting elicited:—

"Our theatrical campaign opened on Monday evening, with every promise of success, as it introduced to a Wexford audience the celebrated African Roscius, Mr. Aldridge, who appeared as Zanga, in Young's celebrated tragedy of *The Revenge*. We cannot, indeed, find language sufficiently strong to do justice to this inimitable actor. His opening scene was powerful and affecting, and at once proved to his admiring auditory his just conception of the difficult character he had to sustain. In the third act, when he worked up Alonzo to the assassination of his friend Don Carlos, by planting in his heart the seeds of jealousy, the manner in which he delivered the few lines, ending with 'to tread upon the Greek and Roman names,' was electrical; and in the last act, where he had completely wrought his victim to his fiendish and hellish purpose, in order to satiate his revenge; and saw Alonzo prostrate—his hellish joy—the self-satisfaction at the wish of destruction he caused—bespoke at once the genius of this mighty actor. During the whole of the last scene there was a breathless silence in the house—so anxious was every-one to hear every word he uttered, and pay that respect which transcendent merit deserves. This gentleman is tall in stature, stoutly built, with a strong caste of face of the African mould; his action is most graceful and becoming; his pronunciation clear and distinct, with a deep and mellow tone of voice; in short, Nature has stamped this man as an actor of the first order. The other characters of the play were most respectably sustained by the company. The evening's entertainments concluded with the farce of *The Padlock*: the part of Mungo by the African Roscius. Here again did we experience a new scene of delight upon his impersonation of this character. If the author of the piece were alive, and after seeing our hero in it, he would say—'that is the man for whom I wrote the piece.' Suffice it to say, he is the first Mungo in the British dominions. The only way to appreciate the character of this man, and to estimate his towering genius, is to go to the theatre and see him. Our old and respected favourite, Mr. J.W. Potter, who is the manager, deserves well of the Wexford people for introducing to them this celebrated character—we trust he will be well repaid for his exertion by full attendance at the theatre during his stay."

The following season Mr. Aldridge returned to Dublin, and, after going through his limited round of characters, acted in a translation of Schiller's *Fiesco*, by General D'Aguillar, which had a good run.

The following is a notice relating to him, which appeared in *Saunders' Dublin News Letter*, January 12, 1833:—

"THEATRE-ROYAL.—Last night, Young's tragedy of *The Revenge* was performed, and the African Roscius played Zanga with a degree of native force and spirit-stirring fidelity that might have made

'Afria and her hundred thrones rejoice,'

could they have beheld their princely representative: his dark features are gifted with an expression that peculiarly fits him for the personation of characters like Zanga, with whose existence all the stronger and darker passions are so closely interwoven, and who are so well described as

'Souls touched with fires, and children of the sun,
With whom revenge is virtue'—

an expression, savage, perhaps, in its origin, and its fiery development, yet conveying sentiments and sensations with a power that 'Europe and her pallid sons' in vain attempt to equal."

At this time M. Laporte, the lessee of the Italian Opera House and Covent Garden, made the African Roscius an offer, which he accepted. His opening was fixed for Wednesday, April 10, 1833; and, after adding to his laurels at Edinburgh, where he played Shylock among other characters, on that night he made his bow for the first time upon the boards of the great "patent theatre," Covent Garden. *The Standard* of April 14, 1833, thus alludes to the circumstance:—

"THEATRE-ROYAL, COVENT GARDEN.—We made a point of being present, for the last three evenings, to witness the performance of that singularly-gifted actor, the African Roscius, who is the first performer of colour that ever appeared on the boards of any theatre in Britain. He had chosen the part of Othello for his first appearance—an undertaking which at present was most hazardous; but, notwithstanding the impression which the inimitable Kean has created in this character, and the genius by which lie has made it peculiarly his own, the result showed that the African Roscius was fully justified in making the bold attempt. We at once gladly express our unqualified delight with his delineation of this masterpiece of the divine Shakespeare. To attempt a minute description would be as superfluous as difficult; he succeeded in deeply affecting the feelings of his audience, and the representation all through was watched with an intense stillness, almost approaching to awe. At the conclusion, the African Roscius was called for by the unanimous acclamation of the whole house, who, upon his appearance, rose *en masse* to receive him with bursts of applause, waving of hats, handkerchiefs, (etc., etc. The *debutant*, evidently deeply affected, expressed his grateful thanks in a very modest and feeling manner, and retired amidst enthusiastic cheering."

Nothing could have been more complete than his success. But there were circumstances against him, and he lost the immediate benefit to which that success entitled him, whilst others, with only half as much, have prospered. The fact of his having appeared as Othello two successive nights before a London audience is one evidence of his triumph, but it was not lasting. The tide of fortune was in his favour, but not "taken at its flood," and hostile and adverse breezes set in to keep him back. Theatres were not doing well, and the "legitimate" business was particularly low. lie performed but four nights at Covent Garden; and then his name was withdrawn from the bills. This sudden and extraordinary termination to what was an unequivocal realization of all that could have been hoped of him, may be variously accounted for. M. Laporte was himself capricious, and a manager's motives, aims, plans, contrivances, impulses, decisions, and arrangements, are all his own. The public can seldom see or comprehend them; and managers are very often at a loss to account to themselves for what they do, while to the looker-on their conduct is, in nine cases out of ten, inexplicable. Certain of the public press—a few individuals—were inimical to the histrionic pretensions of the African. There was but little opportunity for assailing him directly and seriously, for in this country men must give something like a reason for what they say in earnest. Ridicule, however, is within the reach of the most unscrupulous and unthinking, and where it *can* be applied, nothing is more effective. Miss Ellen Tree was the Desdemona of Mr. Aldridge's Othello, and certain admirers of that lady, (who was then unmarried, and, as now, a special favourite), were envious of the Moor's familiarity with her fair face, and ridiculed his privilege. Burnt cork and grease, an imitative and dirty dye, upon a tallowy skin, were, in their fastidious and jaundiced eye, unobjectionable as compared with a veritable and natural hue of our Creator's own painting. Men, who have since grown older, and, if we may judge from their literary pursuits, wiser, took a pleasure in scoffing at "the idea" of "a nigger" filling an intellectual character, and surpassing themselves among others in his delineation of poetry, pathos, and passion. It was "the idea" alone which warped their better taste and judgment, for in reality there was nothing to mock. Had Laporte persisted in his undertaking, Mr. Aldridge would soon have been established as a generally known, popular, and extraordinary actor; but he did nothing of the kind. Prejudices, too, will come even across the great Atlantic.

"Cœlum non animum mutant qui trans mare currunt."

And of this fact Mr. Aldridge has been repeatedly reminded upon coming in contact with actors from the United States. They have been ready to forget the immeasurable distance between themselves and the man of colour, physiologically considering one and the other, and, although engaged to perform minor parts to his more prominent ones, they have had the effrontery to assume the hectoring practised upon "Pompeys" in their own country (a kind of bearing at once contemptibly dictatorial and vulgarly familiar), as though they had luckily fallen upon an object so void of self-respect and self-defence, that they may for once indulge in their nationality with impunity. Mr. Aldridge, however, has been too long admired and patronized in Great Britain, and too long absent from "the country of his early adoption," to submit to or tolerate the slightest Yankeeism of *that* kind, lie is perfectly conscious of his own moral and physical powers as compared with those of men who would avail themselves of the mere force of prejudice to "put him down"; and the quiet dignity of manners, gentlemanly address, and deportment of the African, seldom fail to check conduct the very reverse—as is usually the case among men; for, let everybody use his own weapon, and the polished and best-tempered has the advantage, especially in a cool hand.

American actors, and some actors who have been in America, to this very day, scoff at the African

"Because he is black,"

while they themselves are but little admired for all their whiteness. We can very easily understand the latent animosity and open hostility that one performer feels for and shows to another, according to the circumstances which call forth such sentiments; but we have more difficulty in accounting for the unprovoked, uncharitable, unreasonable, and unjustifiable attacks made upon an individual by educated men whose interests can never clash with his, whose profession teaches liberality, and whose principal boast is strict impartiality. But there are many mysteries as to theatrical criticism that puzzle the uninitiated. Be that as it may, the respectable portion of the press, with one consent, extolled the African Roscius during his exceedingly brief engagement at Covent Garden.

Our hero went straight from Covent Garden to the Surrey Theatre, upon which occasion the following announcement in the playbills heralded his appearance there:—

"Mr. Aldridge, a native of Senegal, and known by the appellation of "The African Roscius!" is engaged at this theatre for two nights; and will have the honour of making his first appearance on Monday next, April 22, in Shakespeare's play of *Othello*. N.B.— The circumstance of a man of colour performing Othello, on the British Stage, is, indeed, an epoch in the history of theatricals; and the honour conferred upon him, in being called for last week, at Covent Garden Theatre, after the performance, by the unanimous voice of the audience, to receive their tribute of applause, is as highly creditable to the native talent of the sunny climes of Africa, as to the universal liberality of a British Public."

There he likewise performed *Oroonoko*, Alambra, in *Paul and Virginia*, Mungo, and other characters. His stay at the Surrey Theatre was not long.

Mr. Aldridge then again left London, and with an improved reputation, lie had stood the test of a London audience, and had not failed; and his value was enhanced among country managers.

No performer has ever enjoyed more local celebrity than Mr. Aldridge has obtained from the period of his quitting the metropolis to this present period of his return to it. From time to time critiques of his performances, setting forth the excellence of his natural and acquired abilities, have reached London, and his name has become familiar to all who take any interest in theatrical matters. Again and again lie visited all the principal towns in the United Kingdom, increasing in popularity wherever he appeared. A file of bills containing his performances, and newspapers containing criticisms upon them, is before us: these are so many repeated evidences of his continuous successes. The one announcing how—

The singular novelty of an actor of colour, personating the routine of Moorish and African characters, has rendered the performances of the African Roscius highly attractive in the theatres in which he has appeared; and the mighty plaudits with which he had uniformly been honoured by crowded audiences, evince the estimation in which his talents are held by the public

—and the other, eulogizing his various efforts in such terms as the following, which we take—as the landlady, in the song, took the nose of her guest—

'As a sample for all the rest.'

TIPPERARY THEATRICALS

THE AFRICAN ROSCIUS AND AMATEURS

This highly-gifted individual, Mr. Aldridge, the celebrated African Roscius has been sojourning in Tipperary for the last week, and has received from the inhabitants of the town generally, as well as of the surrounding country, a tribute of respect seldom tendered to any of the Thespian fraternity. But we do not evince any degree of surprise at Mr. Aldridge's warm reception in Tipperary—that town has always been celebrated for its love of the Drama, for its admiration and encouragement of the talents of any eminent performer, and the due appreciation of their merits. In the present instance we hesitate not in saying that, as a representative of the "Great Avon Bard," Mr. Aldridge in few characters has ever been excelled—nor in his just conception of the writings of that immortal poet have any of his predecessors shown so perfect an intimacy with, or so deep a knowledge of, the intentions of the great dramatist. On the boards, as the personator of the avaricious Shylock, the jealous Othello, or the vengeful Zanga, in Dr. Young's *Revenge*, he has no competitor, and we may justly say, in Shakespeare's words,

"We ne'er shall look upon his like again."

In private life, the pleasing and happy manners—the gentle and unassuming deportment—the suavity and grace with which Mr. Aldridge is endowed—have won for him many friends, whose esteem will, we trust, be as permanent as his theatrical fame will be preeminently lasting.

As the above is an Irish tribute, let us extract a few lines from the more cool, calculating, and matter-of-fact Scotch.

The *Caledonian Mercury*, of March 20, 1833, contains the following remarks:—

We had the pleasure last night of being present at the representation of *Othello* by the celebrated African Roscius, and were at once surprised and delighted with the originality and beauty of his reading of the jealous Moor—whether in the passages which are distinguished by feeling or passion—he showed a command over the sympathies of his auditors, which none but an actor of the first order is possessed of. He reminded us of Kean in many of his best passages, and when time may have deprived us of that great master, the African Roscius will not be an unworthy successor. He was loudly applauded in all his points by a crowded and very fashionable audience, among whom we perceived many of the most eminent literary and professional characters in the city.

A score of other Scotch papers spoke of him in similar terms. Like the great Garrick, we find him equally happy in deepest tragedy and broadest farce. In the former, he is even Richard the Third and Bertram (we don't see a Romeo—a character, by the way, Edmund Kean could not personate); in the latter, he is, among other *suitable* characters— (this is not meant as a pun)—Jim Crow, Ginger Blue, the Virginian Mummy, singing nigger songs and dancing nigger dances, and now then giving lectures in defence of the Drama, in such language as the following, which we copy from a report:—

Bigotry and fanaticism have excited themselves in all possible shapes to annoy the professors of the dramatic art; but, fortunately for the honour of the Stage and dignity of human nature, it has found patrons and friends in the persons of the greatest and most learned men in the most enlightened periods of the world's history. Nothing can more strongly prove the importance of dramatic amusements than the diametrically opposite opinions that have been entertained upon the subject—opinions that have uniformly run like parallel lines for centuries—unbending, and without the smallest inclination to converge. From a reflecting mind, this view of it alone must claim the most serious investigation. Sculpture, painting, and music, are still cherished, and have also been appreciated and esteemed commendable by all, with the miserable exception of the *most ignorant*; and the Drama, when viewed in its proper light, will stand as high as the loftiest of the arts and sciences. Like every other art and science, however, profession or trade, it has its opponents and its enemies. Among these are many who argue for their opinions on fair, reasonable, and honourable terms. There is also another class, twenty times more numerous, more inimical, but less injurious, to the cause of the Drama than the first, and this last class, founded their animosity on a basis of folly, ignorance, and bigotry, combine in crying it down with the utmost avidity and bitterness. It has also, along with its truly great and eloquent supporters, many unthinking, ill-judging, and ill-advised friends, such as are common in every state, station, business, and degree of life, whose ill-digested arguments in its favour are more destructive to its success than otherwise, and, consequently, are of that description which, as Hamlet says, "would be much more honoured in the breach than the observance." Luther, upon most subjects, would be attended to with respect, if not conviction, and one would imagine his view of the Stage alone would induce the serious part of the community to attend to the directions of the Stage, not to its destruction. He says, in comedies, particularly those of the Roman writers, the duties of the various situations of life are held out to view, and, as it were, reflected from a mirror. The office of parents and the proper conduct of children are faithfully delineated, and, what to young men may be advantageous, the vices and characters of profligate women are exhibited in their true colours; excellent lessons given to them how they should conduct themselves towards virtuous women in courtship; strong exhortations to matrimony are brought forward, without which no state, no government, can subsist.

We find him acting in plays written expressly for him, with gentlemen amateurs, and, at fashionable watering-places, among, and patronised by, select assemblies. Amidst a mass of testimonials to his public and private worth, are letters written by such distinguished individuals as the following:—

Sir D. Brewster, Principal of St. Andrew's College, to Professor Fleming, King's College, Aberdeen.
The Right Hon. the Earl of Chesterfield to the Marquis of Waterford.
The Hon. the Provost of Wick.
E. M'Ivor, Esq., Banker, to George Murray, Esq., Provost of Tain.
Miss O'Neill.
Madame Malibran.
Mrs. Hannyngton, of Dungannon Castle, to Captain Algeo.
President of Clongowes College.
President of Carlow College.
Mrs. Lyons, to Mrs. Bond, of Derricor Castle.
The Hon. the Provost of Dundalk.
The Rev. Michael Coghlan.
Alexander Gair, Esq., Banker, Tain, to P. M'Lachlan, Esq., Wick.
His Grace the Archbishop of Tuam.

All of whom commend and recommend him in the strongest possible terms We extract a couple of the most important:—

Manchester, April 18, 1834

MADAME MALIBRAN presents her grateful respects and compliments to the African Roscius, for the high treat afforded her last night, in his intellectual personation of *Othello*. Madame Malibran never witnessed, in the course of her professional career in both hemispheres, a more interesting and powerful performance, marked throughout by that strict adherence to nature which should be the characteristic of every dramatic portraiture. In returning the volume so kindly lent by Mr. Aldridge, she begs to tender her best thanks and sincere wishes for his continued success.

The *Clonmel Advertiser* says:—

After the great concurrence of the United Kingdom having acknowledged him to be the greatest actor of the present age, we feel it perfectly unnecessary for us to oiler a single recommendatory remark in his favour; it would be, in fine, as much a work of supererogation, as if we were "to gild refined gold." We feel extreme pleasure, notwithstanding, in placing upon public record the opinion given of him, on a very recent occasion, by Lady Wrixon Beecher, late Miss O'Neill:—"I have seen him in Cheltenham and Cork, and, during my professional as well as private life, I never saw so correct a 'portraiture of Othello' amidst the principal luminaries of my day. It is true Kean reserved himself for particular passages, which were made to tell with startling effect; but, as a whole, his performance was not superior to the Roscius, whose acting, throughout, is transcendently uniform."

Among other high compliments that have been paid him, the House of Representatives of St. Domingo passed an unanimous vote in 1838, complimenting him on his successful progress in contradicting the assertion that his race is incapable of mental culture, and bestowing upon him a commission, with the rank of Captain, and Aide-de-Camp Extraordinary to his Excellency the (then) President Boyer. This honour was delivered to Mr. Aldridge through the consul in London. Many addresses have been written for him, and to him. From among the former we extract the following clever poetic effusion, from the pen of Mr. Stirling Coyne, a dramatic author of some metropolitan celebrity—one who has contributed largely to the best productions of the Adelphi, and the writer of its latest successful pieces:—

ADDRESS

"Othello's occupation's gone!"—'tis o'er;
The mask has fall'n—I'm actor here no more.
*But still your pupil—**protégé**—whate'er*
Your kindness made me, and your fostering care,
"This mourning suit" perchance offends your sight;
But Nature triumphs, and asserts her right;
Expands my heart, and bids my tongue explain
The pride—the gratitude that swells each vein,
That floods unseen my dusky cheek—and dwells
Enshrin'd within my bosom's deepest cells;
"Nurs'd in the land, where rolls the giant tide,
*Of sluggish **Senegal**, through deserts wide,*
Where every tainted breeze comes winged with death,
And Nature sickens in the poison breath;
Amid such scenes the Negro strays alone
In happy innocence—untaught—unknown:
Happy because that desert's faithless sand
He claims his own, his long-loved native land.
But soon the white man comes, allured by gain,
O'er his free limbs fling slavery's galling chain;
Robs him of heaven's best gift—and casts him then
Forth from his equal rank with fellow-men;
Transforms him to a brute—or worse—a slave:
Who loathes to bear the life that Nature gave.
Oh! Justice heaven;—but list, the time is nigh:
Freedom approaches from the western sky—
Sheds her bright glory tow'rd the Indian Seas,
And shakes her banner o'er the Carribees.
The tortured black man hears her thrilling voice,
And checks his groans one moment to rejoice:
Forgive me, generous friends, nor rashly deem;
My tongue too long has lingered on this theme.
You, who have long loved liberty so well,
The strong emotions of my soul can tell.

But there's a warmer, deeper feeling here,
Which gushes like the desert waters, clear:
That fount is gratitude—it flows for you
To whom the tribute of my thanks is due;
You, who espousing injured Afric's cause,
First cheered my efforts by your kind applause;
O'er look'd my errors, taught my mind to soar,
And op'd my path to England's genial shore.
Though we must part, my best protectors, still
My heart will cherish till its pulse is still.
Its proudest record—the fresh memory,
That here the sable African was free
From every bond—save those which kindness threw
Around his heart—and bound it fast to you.

This was spoken upon his leaving Dublin to appear at Covent Garden. In the midst of his provincial career, however, but while he was resting for a while upon his well-earned laurels, the following paragraph went the round of the papers:—

Death of The African Roscius

A melancholy and fatal accident occurred to Mr. Aldridge, the African Roscius, last week. Mr. Aldridge was returning in his carriage from the seat of Colonel Powell, when, within half a mile of Llandillo, one of the horses took fright at the blaze of light from the iron-works with which the county is studded; this occurred on the brink of a precipice, over which the carriage swerved with its inmate, dragging the horses and postilion. The footman had a most providential escape. He was in the act of alighting to seize the horses' heads as the carriage was precipitated over the cliff. It is needless to add, that Mr. Aldridge, the postilion, and the horses were killed on the spot—the carriage being dashed to atoms. The place where this frightful accident occurred is one hundred and twenty from the summit to the bottom.

The success of a hoax of the above kind depends more upon its apparent seriousness than evident probability, and the particulars of "the melancholy and fatal accident" were so gravely and minutely set forth, that nobody doubted them. The author knew well how to lie, but we do not envy him his merit, nor the satisfaction he derived from his vicious invention. In all probability, he was a Yankee who forged the falsehood, for such hoaxes have come from that country until the cry of "Wolf!" would not be believed in this, were it ever so well founded. Mr. Aldridge, however, was not injured by the groundless report in question. On the contrary, it made his name the more known, increased the interest which those who knew him took in his welfare, and served as a strong advertisement in widely circulating his fame. In time it became generally known that the African Roscius was alive and still prospering; and, coming to a later date, such notices as the following appeared, which we quote from *The Era*, a London weekly newspaper, which regularly reports all the theatrical business of the provinces:—

"The African Roscius, Mr. Aldridge, performs during the next week at Richmond. Those of the metropolis who have a wish to witness his acting, with a view to engaging him, have now an opportunity of so doing, as he will appear in *Othello*, and other characters which have gained him a great celebrity throughout the provinces. All the local papers, without one exception, describe him as an actor of extraordinary talent, both in tragic and comic business, and it is said, we believe with truth, that his appearance on a London stage would be very attractive."

Mr. Aldridge never abandoned the desire of making himself generally known and popular in London. To that end he has studied deeply and laboured long in his profession. The lapse of some years had wiped him from the memories of the comparative few who had seen him act in the metropolis, and curiosity concerning him was very often expressed. Not unconscious of his only natural disadvantage—that of his colour, he waited, with characteristic modesty, the invitation to appear again, to which his provincial reputation entitled him; but the legitimate Drama has been long at a discount. One or two managers lacked, to say the least of it, the moral courage to engage him, when opportunity occurred. The success of Mr. Brooke, however, at the Olympic, a gentleman with whom Mr. Aldridge had often acted in the country, drew him nearer London, and the management of the Surrey Theatre having offered him tempting terms, he accepted them, and his name again figured "on the Surrey side."

We believe that, notwithstanding the entire absence of all that bad taste and worse feeling which were displayed in certain comments, which, during his previous visit, reflected more upon his race and their Creator than Mr. Aldridge himself, and, on the other hand, the high encomiums that the press bestowed upon him, his appearance at the Surrey this time has been attended with some disappointment. In the first place, the house is itself essentially a veritable "minor," whatever be the performers or performances introduced there. In the second place, the management evinced no spirit in bringing him forward. There were neither advertisements, placards, nor posters, to announce the fact, nor any stir made to circulate it, while those who "supported him" ranted so as to mar one moment the interest excited by Mr. Aldridge in another. Yet his usual share of commendation was given him.

The following are extracts from notices of Mr. Aldridge's acting, which have appeared in different newspapers upon this his latest appearance before a London audience:—

From the *Morning Post*, March 21, 1848:

Mr. Ira Aldridge is a *bonâ fide* African, of mulatto tint, with woolly hair; his features are capable of much expression, his action is unrestrained and picturesque, and his voice clear, full, and resonant. It was interesting to witness the acting of Mr. Ira Aldridge, a native of Africa, giving utterance to the wrongs of his race in his assumed character, and standing in an attitude of triumph over the body of one of its oppressors. Mr. Ira Aldridge is an intelligent actor, and his elocutionary powers are admirable. Compared with the people by whom he was last night surrounded, he might with strict justice be considered a true Roscius.

From the *Morning Herald*, of March 22, 1848:

A mulatto, of the name of Aldridge, appeared on Monday night at the Surrey Theatre, in the character of Zanga, meeting with all the success which cleverness and considerable experience would be likely to ensure. Mr. Aldridge is evidently a man of intelligence, and his personation of the revengeful hero of Young's disagreeable tragedy was discriminative, energetic, and disfigured by no clumsinesses or incongruities of elocution. He was loudly applauded; and upon being called before the curtain, propitiated the countenance of the audience in a neat and well-turned address. He afterwards appeared in *The Padlock*—playing the part of Mungo with much drollery.

From the *Morning Advertiser*, March 21, 1848:

He achieved complete success, and it is nothing more than justice to his merits to say he deserved it. He has a clear and flexible voice, which he uses with great judgment and taste; he can infuse great expression and feeling into his intonation; his emphasis is judicious; and his transitions natural and appropriate. His acting was excellent throughout. Without attempting to institute a comparative criticism between the performance or merits of this gentleman and any of those who might be considered to be his competitors, we may venture to say that he stands, without question, in the first class. In the farce of *The Padlock*, his performance of the part of Mungo was equal to anything we ever witnessed, displaying great humour and histrionic art in setting forth the salient points of that very facetious specimen of sable servants. The greatest applause accompanied his efforts. If this gentleman has assigned to him characters equally well calculated to call forth his abilities, he cannot fail to be a great acquisition to the theatre, and to attract good houses, which, after all, is the great desideratum in these cases.

From the *London Telegraph*, March 29, 1848:

A native-born African appearing on our Stage is somewhat of a curiosity in histrionic annals; and it afforded us a pleasing proof of the wearing away of that prejudice against men of a colour different from our own, which has long lurked in the hearts of nearly all of us, that Mr. Aldridge, the "African Roscius," who on Monday night performed the part of Othello at this theatre, was, by a numerous and respectable audience, most favourably received. Mr. Aldridge's impersonation of the brave man who loved "not wisely but too well," is a treat of a high order. With the similitude of country and complexion, the illusion becomes exceedingly strong, whilst the critic has not to object to a defective knowledge of the language in which our great dramatist originally introduced this splendid conception. In the expression of love, rage, jealousy, and despair, this performance presented the skill of a consummate knowledge of the human passions, wrought, as it were, to a powerful and fearful reality, From the first moment in which the poison of jealousy taints his heart, till the "green-eyed monster" marked him for its own, in the progress of the passion, its deep workings, until he raged in the convulsions of agonising thoughts and convictions, the interest never flagged for a moment. Some passages merit the warmest praise, amongst which we may select the pathetic reference to his personal disadvantages. The scene in which Iago first attempts to excite his jealousy, when as yet "He doubts—yet doats—suspects, yet strongly loves," and the solemn impressiveness with which he declares, "I had rather be a toad and live upon the vapour of a dungeon, etc."

There was no clap-tap, no rant, even in the most vigorous and impassioned scenes; but truth to nature, and a just conception of character, were evidenced throughout.

From the *Sunday Times*, March 26, 1848:

His delineation of the proud, revengeful Moor was finely conceived, and executed with great dramatic effect. In the soliloquies, and those passages in which the reflective powers of the mind are at work, while the material action is suspended, he possesses the rare faculty of completely abstracting and separating himself from all external objects, or of only receiving impressions from those that harmonise with the state of his mind. Zanga's opening soliloquy in the first act, during the storm, expresses this mental condition very forcibly. In scenes of emotion Mr. Aldridge is exceedingly natural; his grief and joy seem to spring directly from his heart, and have a contagious influence upon his audience. Nothing could have been more admirably pourtrayed than the exultation of Zanga when he finds that his schemes for the destruction of Alonzo are ripening to success. There is a mad intoxication in his joy—an intensity in his savage delight that is scarcely less terrible than his rage. Of the better feelings of our nature we have but few indications in the character of the Moor brooding over his long-cherished vengeance; occasionally, however, we have touches of humanity gleaming athwart the dark picture, which were elicited with great effect by Mr. Aldridge. The remembrance of his father's death and his country's wrongs, and his own degradation, which had burned into his heart, is obliterated when he beholds his enemy lifeless at his feet, and the late remorse of a noble heart was expressed with deep feeling and pathos, when he exclaims—

> *"And art thou dead? So is my enmity—*
> *I war not with the dust."*

As regards his general delineation of the Moor's character, it was marked by careful study and judicious conception. Mr. Aldridge played the part of the Negro servant with extraordinary humour and natural drollery. The childlike simplicity of the Negro character—easily excited to mirth or sorrow—with its love of fun and mischief, were admirably pourtrayed by him.

From the *Dispatch*, March 26, 1848:

Mr. Ira Aldridge, a gentleman of colour, appeared last week as Zanga, in *The Revenge*, and deservedly met with warm encouragement. He is an actor of talent; and in such characters as Zanga can make a very deep impression. He has power to present, in strong, broad, effective bearing, the injuries, sufferings, and passions of the much-abused African. In a totally different character, that of Mungo, in *The Padlock*, seldom, or ever, played by a native of the torrid zone, he displayed considerable *vis comica*.

Bell's Life in London, of March 26, 1848, writes, it will be seen, *in precisely the same words* as the *Morning Advertiser* of the 21st:

Mr. Ira Aldridge has a clear and flexible voice, which he uses with great judgment and taste; he can infuse great expression and feeling into his intonation; his emphasis is judicious; and his transitions natural and appropriate. His acting was excellent throughout. Without attempting to institute a comparative criticism between the performance or merits of this gentleman and any of those who might he considered to be his competitors, we may venture to say that he stands, without question, in the first class. In the farce of *The Padlock*, his performance of the part of Mungo was equal to anything we ever witnessed, displaying great humour and histrionic art in setting forth the salient points of that very facetious specimen of sable servants. The greatest applause accompanied his efforts. If this gentleman has assigned to him characters equally well calculated to call forth his abilities, he cannot fail to be a great acquisition to the theatre, and to attract good houses, which, after all, is the great desideratum in these cases.

From the *Weekly Times*, March 26, 1848:

Mr. Ira Aldridge is a *bonâ fide* African, of mulatto tint, with woolly hair; his features are capable of much expression, his action is unrestrained and picturesque, and his voice clear, full, and resonant. His powers of energetic declamation are very marked, and the whole of his acting appears impulsed by a current of feeling of no inconsiderable weight and vigour, yet controlled and guided in a manner that clearly shows the actor to be a person of much study and great Stage experience.

From the *Observer*, March 26, 1848:

Mr. Aldridge has a clear and flexible voice, which he uses with great judgment and taste; he knows how to infuse considerable expression and feeling into his intonation; his emphasis is judicious; and his transitions were natural and appropriate. Without attempting to institute a comparative criticism between the performance or merits of this gentleman and any of those who might be considered to be his competitors, we may venture to say that he stands, without question, in a high class. In the farce of *The Padlock*, his performance of the part of Mungo was excellent, displaying great humour and histrionic art in setting forth the salient points of that very facetious specimen of sable servants.

From the *Era*, March 26, 1848:

On Monday (March 20, 1848), Mr. Aldridge, "The African Roscius," who has gained a great celebrity in the provinces, appeared at this house in the opposite characters of Zanga, in Young's tragedy of *The Revenge*, and Mungo, in the farce of *The Padlock*. This was not Mr. Aldridge's first bow to a London audience. Some years ago, he performed two nights running as Othello, at Covent Garden, and afterwards went through several parts at the Surrey. He was at that time very young, and has since, by continual practice, improved himself in every respect as an actor. He was, however, highly successful when he last appeared in London. The papers spoke of his performance in terms of unequivocal commendation; but, notwithstanding the novelty of a man of colour representing Shakespeare's intellectual heroes so as to meet the serious approval of critics, and the extraordinary circumstance of Mr. Aldridge (although a black) taking his stand in the profession as a gentleman and a scholar, capable of receiving the poet's creations, and pourtraying his thoughts in a display of histrionic art—notwithstanding the general approval he met with, and the encouragement he ought to have received, he made but little way as an actor of great pretensions, and soon disappeared from the London boards. Ridicule had something to do with this. The disadvantage of colour, which excluded him from all chance of success in America, was not entirely overcome in England among a prejudiced, wanton, and unthinking few, who could not let an opportunity pass for sneering at and ridiculing the "presumptuous nigger." One publication in particular, now out of print, was particularly unmerciful, and its lampoons were sadly discouraging to the tenacious young "Roscius," for ridicule does not always blunt the feelings of those against whom it is directed, but, on the contrary, often makes them more susceptible.

Mr. Aldridge, however, is, in our opinion, likely to outlive such petty attacks as he was then subjected to.

His appearance at the Surrey has been promising in the extreme, and we think his London engagements this time will be both gratifying and profitable to him. He is a very excellent actor. Like all of his race, and his country itself, he is one of extremes. The earnestness of seriousness is equal to the heartiness of his mirth. As Zanga he is exceedingly fine, looking the character of the Moor to perfection, and acting it with great power and correctness. For the tragedy itself we have little regard. It was written when mere declamation was admired, and the College critic sat in the pit to applaud stilted language, which is now looked upon as so much grammatical nonsense. Still there are some stirring passages in *The Revenge*, and some melodramatic situations, and of these Mr. Aldridge avails himself very effectively. It was interesting to mark the subdued tone and superior acting of the African, as compared with the wild and unmeaning rant of those who "supported" him. In his passionate deliveries he received much applause, and upon those occasions his voice rises to ringing, clear, and distinct accents, while at others he speaks in a measured and grave style, almost too sober to be in keeping with the fiery nature of the Moor. We look upon him as an extraordinary personage, and quite a curiosity to those who take any interest in the physiology of man. In farce he is exceedingly funny. You see the veritable nigger, whose good-nature, humour, and even wit, are so commonly ridiculed. As Mungo he is very amusing, giving way to his absurdity with all the zest of one of his colour. Mr. Aldridge sings, too, and his "Possum up a Gum-tree" is one of the funniest things that can be imagined. No mock "Ethiopian Serenader" could come near it. It is novel to see one who has been obtaining much applause in pourtraying passion in its most poetic shape, descend to the broad farce of mock drunkenness, and cramming into his capacious mouth a lighted candle, which he mistakes for the neck of a bottle in the other hand; and it is only a man of natural genius who can do both so as to be commended for the faithfulness of his mimicry. On Monday next, Mr. Aldridge will appear as Othello, a character for which he is so peculiarly fitted. We are inclined to believe that he will be very attractive as the "darky husband" of the fair Desdemona. We advise the anti-slavery people, who visit Exeter Hall upon great occasions, to see Mr. Aldridge at the Surrey. His appearance there is a "great moral lesson" in favour of anti-slavery.

Again, on April 8, 1848, the *Era* says:

There is a repose, a dignity, and a natural gravity and earnestness about Mr. Aldridge's personification of the dusky Moor that are particularly impressive. He is very fine in the part, and the natural hue of his skin helps to make the illusion perfect. There is much originality, too, about the African's delineation of the character. His declamation has all the dignity, and his action all the grace, which belong to primitive races. Nor is he wanting in that refinement without which there is but little to admire in man, as he appears before the more civilized of his species. Mr. Aldridge is something more than an African: he is a scholar and a gentleman; at least, he acts like one. In *Othello*, he delivers the most difficult passages with a degree of correctness that surprises the beholder, and, at times, he ascends to a pourtrayal of the conflicting passions of the jealous husband in a manner both artistical and true. The workings of his mind, and sensations of his heart, were conspicuous in his swarthy visage, and depicted in every gesture. After the death of Desdemona, when he awoke to a consciousness of the deception that had been practised upon him, in the frenzy of his remorse he lifted the lifeless body of his murdered and wronged wife from the bed, as though she had been an infant. There was something terribly touching in this display of physical strength, wrought up by mental agony.

From the *Illustrated London News* (with an engraving of the African Roscius as Zanga, in *The Revenge*):

Mr. Aldridge possesses an excellent voice, commanding figure, and expressive countenance; to which he adds the advantages of education and study. His dress, which is novel and picturesque, reminds one of the portraits of Abd-el-Kader. Throughout the play he more than realized the high encomiums that had previously been passed upon him; and many who ridiculed the idea of a native-born African successfully representing a dramatic character, retired with very different feelings. Nor is his talent confined to tragedy. His representation of Mungo, in *The Padlock*, is a laughable performance, differing entirely from the Ethiopian absurdities we have been taught to look upon as correct portraitures; his total *abandon* is very amusing. He reappeared on the 27th as Othello, with great success.

From Douglas Jerrold's Newspaper, of March 25, 1848:

On Monday, Mr. Aldridge, a Negro, performed the part of Zanga, and although the selection of such an individual looked like the parading a piece of reality, by having a real black man to represent the ideal character, and, therefore, seemed to be an insufferable piece of vulgarity, yet we thought it our duty to witness it. We were agreeably disappointed. Mr. Aldridge is an undoubted Negro, but is gifted with an intelligence of perception, dignity of action, and force of expression, that not only do honour to his particular race, but to humanity. He reads with much feeling and appreciation of the author; and there is a force and vigour in his passionate enunciation that is stirring, and perfectly free from imitation or rant. He especially possesses a freedom of gait and natural dignity of movement, derivable probably from the unconfined nature of his early life. He has nothing of the savage, but his freedom from the petty manners of conventional training. He made as much of Zanga as it is possible to do of so wordy, blustering, and clumsy an Iago. He has a slight foreign accent, and his voice, like most of his countrymen, is thin in the upper tones. He immediately afterwards performed Mungo, in *The Padlock*, and with so much humour, and with such characteristic songs, that it gave universal satisfaction, and it is doubtful whether his *forte* be not rather comedy than tragedy. It is certain he is a man of no mean amount of talent, and its range is considerable, as is proved by his clever delineation alike of Zanga and Mungo. He was enthusiastically received by a very excellent house, and we are quite sure his complexion will be no impediment to his receiving the applause due to his merit.

The Satirist, of April 2, 1848, says:

The African Roscius continues to draw good houses at the Surrey, from the novelty of seeing "a real black," and the more especially a tragic actor, which Mr. Aldridge is, beyond all doubt. His Othello is a very superior piece of acting, well considered, and well developed; the latter part, where, after the death of Desdemona, he becomes conscious of her innocence, his desperation, and the abandoning of himself to the furies of his mind, were touches of the highest excellence. As an actor he has fought his way through every opposition and prejudice, and as a foreigner and a stranger comes to England to delineate the poetic conceptions of England's bard.

Other London papers speak of Mr. Aldridge in similar terms. Upon the principle of "what everybody says must be true," Mr. Aldridge must be a man of no ordinary talent. As a whole his performances are, according to every testimony that has been given in reference to them, extraordinarily line, whatever may be the occasional objections that spring up in the minds of those who endeavour to find faults in them. He is, however, before a public who will judge for themselves; that they admire his efforts is very evident in the encouragement he receives, and that his various and peculiar merits may be more generally known and tested, this brief history of his life and labours has been written.

The African, notwithstanding all that has been said of him, has yet to be brought fairly and completely before the London public, by whom he is, comparatively speaking, unknown. His engagement at the Surrey Theatre has just terminated with offers to renew it; but it is on the Middlesex side the water he must take his stand and be thoroughly tested. *Punch*, seeing a joke and availing himself of it, said lately:—

"*Ira est furor brevis*."—The theatrical critics are loud in praise of areal Ethiopian tragedian, a Mr. Aldridge, with the unusual Christian name of *Ira*, which is, no doubt, symbolical of its owner being "the rage," wherever he goes.

Mr. Aldridge will, no doubt, soon come forward more conspicuously than he has hitherto done, and justify the above remark. At Edinburgh, Mr. W. Murray, the spirited manager of the Theatre Royal, took great pleasure in helping to his successes, while the Scotch people have shown a marked appreciation of his merits. Such has been precisely the case with Mr. Calcraft and the Irish; facts to which Mr. Aldridge refers with lively and mingled sentiments of pride and gratitude.

We have witnessed the performances of Mr. Aldridge, and if testimony to his superior abilities and accomplishments as a tragic and comic actor were wanting, we would readily add our own humble opinion of them. But those qualities are beyond dispute. He possesses every mental and physical requisite for such parts as he fills, and is an ornament to his profession, and a credit, not only to his race in particular, but to society at large, of which he is a bright, albeit a jetty member. In the character of Othello—his special favourite (for he has a decided preference for serious parts)—he seems to have precisely Dr. Johnson's conception of it. That great critic says:—"The fiery openness of Othello, magnanimous, artless, and credulous, boundless in confidence, ardent in his affection, inflexible in his resolution, and obdurate in his revenge, are proofs of Shakspeare's skill in human nature."

Mr. Aldridge feels and acts all this.

In *The Slave*, he is solemn in the intensity of his hatred, bursting out occasionally into a blaze of fierce invective and passionate declamation, and then hiding the fire of his feelings beneath the assumed servility necessary to his purpose and his station. There is no other actor who exhibits the same amount of gravity, save Mr. Macready, who carries his seriousness, to our humble thinking, to an unnatural extreme. Mr. Macready puts on the "in-tense earnestness" and "wrapped fixedness" which belong to greatness of soul, and wears the garments well; but they are evidently borrowed for the occasion, however much they become the wearer, and exhibit his skill in the adjustment of each particular fold. Mr. Aldridge, on the other hand, appears in such robes as though they fell upon him without an effort to possess them, and he wears, as it were, his own by right of inheritance. The dark shades of his face become doubly sombre in their thoughtful aspect; there is something true to nature in the nightlike gloom that is spread over them; an expression more terrible than paler lineaments can assume.

In farce, Mr. Aldridge is funny, as he is serious in tragedy. The ebony becomes polished—the coal emits sparks. His face is the faithful index of his mind, and as there is not a darker frown than his, so is there not a broader grin. The ecstacy of his long shrill note, in "Oppossum up a gum-tree," can only be equalled by the agony of his cry over the body of Desdemona. The sublime and the ridiculous defined, but not blended or confounded one with the other.

With these few general observations upon his acting, we conclude our task—one hastily performed, and shaped out of a handful of loose materials, such as a few old playbills, newspaper notices, and some memoranda that were indispensable. Mr. Aldridge, although aware that a string of such facts as are here set forth, would be calculated to advance his fame and increase public curiosity respecting him, has, with characteristic diffidence, left the entire construction of the narrative to the discretion of the writer, whose comments have been the gratuitous convictions consequent upon the simple facts submitted to him. Should the reader detect what he deems to be remarks too partial, and conclusions one-sided, some allowance, it is hoped, will be made for the bias which the mind naturally receives when engaged upon an undertaking in which its sympathies are excited, and when its approval is justified by the evidence it elicits. We lay down our pen thoroughly persuaded that, even with a set-off thus deducted from the gross amount of favourable construction contained in these pages, Mr. Ira Aldridge, the African Roscius, will, in no respect, be a loser by the interesting truths that remain, and others of his colour may sec occasion to rejoice in their publicity.

The Black Doctor: A Romantic Drama in Four Acts

DRAMATIS PERSONAE

HANNIBAL GRIMAUD, wine shop owner
LIZETTE GRIMAUD, his wife
SUSANNE GRIMAUD, his daughter
PIERRE BRIQUET, valet to St. Luce
JACQUES FILS, suitor to Susanne
CHRISTIAN, old Negro servant to Fabian
FABIAN:, the black doctor
PAULINE REYNERIE, beloved of Fabian
LIA, mulatto servant to Pauline
CHEVALIER ST. LUCE cousin and fiancé to Pauline
MARCHIONESS DE LA REYNERIE, Pauline's mother
ANDRE, loyal friend to Fabian
AURELIA, sister to St. Luce
LORDS, LADIES, SOLDIERS, JAILORS, etc.

Act I

Scene I

(The wine shop of Hannibal Grimaud, *at the town of* St. Louis, *in the Isle of Bourbon. Enter* Grimaud, Lizette, *and* Susanne, *right)*

Hannibal: Don't talk, woman, but hear me! I'm Commander-in-Chief! As the great Louis said, "I'm France"—which means, I'm everything and everybody.

Lizette: But now, husband, consider—

Hannibal: Don't waste your breath by husbanding me! I'm firm, inflexible! A solid square! There's no breaking through me.

Susanne: But, dear father—

Hannibal: Don't father me you jade; or rather, don't get anybody else to father me. I tell you, when you do marry, it shall be to a man of my choosing. Do you imagine that I, Hannibal Grimaud, who have served seventeen campaigns, will condescend to marry my daughter to a common barber?

Lizette: Pierre Briquet isn't a common barber; he keeps as good a shop as any in the town, and is well to do in the world beside.

Hannibal: Not a common barber! Look at my chin; how dare you contradict me? Didn't he shave me yesterday with his own hand?

Susanne: That was out of friendship; for, you know, your own hand shook so with—

Hannibal: Silence, you impudent baggage, or I'll shake you. Once for all, I tell you I'm not to be shaved into any such connections; and as for that other suitor of yours—that threadpaper fellow, Jacques Fils, why, he's a fool.

Lizette: He's as good a young man as any in town.

Hannibal: Good! Good for nothing.

Lizette: Sober, steady and industrious.

Susanne: And an excellent workman.

Lizette: Two such suitors are not to be despised.

Susanne: And I'm sure men are scarce enough in the colony, unless you'd have me marry a blackamoor.

HANNIBAL: You shall marry whom I please, you jade, and he shall be as black as I like. I tell you Pierre Briquet and Jacques Fils are very well in their way; but be prudent, girl; give your best smiles to the best customers. Remember you're a soldier's daughter; and though your post may be a wine shop, let your heart be surrounded with a chevaux de frize of pride, which shall render it impervious to the puffs of a barber, or all the finedrawn compliments of a tailor.

LIZETTE: I'm sure Susanne has all the proper pride of her mother's family.

HANNIBAL: Lather and soapsuds, what do you mean? Why, you were only a laundress when I raised you to the honorable distinction of a soldier's wife! Her mother's family indeed— she has little to boast of on that score.

LIZETTE: Score, indeed! Your washing-score was long enough when I married you, and you were only a—

HANNIBAL: Silence, woman! (*Looking round*) Here comes some neighbors; order, to your post. And remember, I'm commander.

(*Enter* PIERRE BRIQUET *and* JACQUES FILS, *left*)

HANNIBAL: Welcome neighbors, welcome.

PIERRE: Good morning, friend Grimaud; I've some news for you; so just step in, though I'm in a terrible hurry.

HANNIBAL: Ay; good, I hope?

PIERRE: For me, at any rate; but first, some wine; my throat's as dry as the high road.

JACQUES: And so is mine.

HANNIBAL: Susanne, some wine. Ah, this is a fine country.

PIERRE: Do you say so?

HANNIBAL: Ay, for wine's cheap, and one's always thirsty—ha, ha!

ALL: Ha, ha! very cool.

(SUSANNE *brings wine*)

HANNIBAL: Well, Master Briquet, now for your news.

PIERRE: Well, first and foremost, my shop's to let.

SUSANNE: Your shop?

PIERRE: Yes, my shop, pretty one; I'm this very day engaged by the Chevalier St. Luce, as his valet and confidential attendant.

SUSANNE: What! Mademoiselle de la Reynerie's cousin, and who they say is to be her husband?

PIERRE: So they say; and now she's her own mistress, the death of her mother having removed all restraint.

HANNIBAL: But is the death of the Marchioness authenticated?

PIERRE: Why, seeing the vessel she was to have sailed to France in was wrecked, and every soul has perished, there's very little doubt of the matter. Ah, poor Mademoiselle de la Reynerie! She has had two narrow escapes, for grief and anxiety had nearly killed her.

HANNIBAL: Ay, but the Black Doctor saved her both times.

LIZETTE: Only, to think now, that a mulatto, and a slave, should have become the most eminent physician in all the island!

HANNIBAL: The Black Doctor isn't a slave.

LIZETTE: Well, but he was before he was free.

HANNIBAL: Don't you run down people, wife of mine. Remember what you were before I married you.

PIERRE: But the strangest thing of all is, that after the Black Doctor had saved the life of Mademoiselle de la Reynerie, and become domiciled in the family, he should suddenly disappear, and now nearly six months have elapsed since he was seen here in St. Louis, though some of the negroes say he has been observed wandering on the cliffs, but always avoiding anyone who appeared to seek him.

HANNIBAL: Well, everybody likes the Black Doctor, and so they should, if it were only for the services he has rendered Mademoiselle de la Reynerie; she'll be a treasure to the man that wins her.

PIERRE: And she's so rich, too, plenty of gold and jewels; plantations here, and estates in France.

HANNIBAL: Unexceptionable and desirable plunder, friend Briquet, and worth leading a forlorn hope for.

SUSANNE: I suppose we may look soon, then for a wedding?

PIERRE: Why, can't exactly say, though the Chevalier will shortly honor me with his entire confidence, and I'll let you know as soon as we arrange affairs.

(HANNIBAL *goes upstage;* LIZETTE *follows*)

HANNIBAL: We, indeed.

PIERRE I say, Susanne, what pleasure I should have in curling you up for a certain day.

SUSANNE: Curling me up, indeed! What do you mean?

PIERRE: Though art couldn't improve you, Susanne. Macassar oil, bergamot, and eau de Cologne would be only adding perfumery to the violet

SUSANNE: La! Briquet, how you do talk.

JACQUES (*aside, very melancholy*): I see my suit cut on the cross; soft soap carries it.

SUSANNE: What's the matter, Jacques? You seem dull today.

JACQUES (*very spoony*): Not particular.

PIERRE: It's only the thoughts of losing my company, Susanne; quite natural, you know! The needle always inclines to the pole—but I must be off.

JACQUES (*joyfully*): What! Are you going?

PIERRE: Yes, and I'm going to take you with me; you don't think I'd leave you here with Susanne?

JACQUES (*going up*): Heigho!

PIERRE: Besides, I must attend the Chevalier; he will be expecting me. Goodbye, Susanne, I shall see you again soon; good day, Grimaud; good day Madame Grimaud.

HANNIBAL: If you hear any news of the Black Doctor, mind you let us know.

PIERRE: It's likely I shall; for little Lia, the foster sister of Mademoiselle de la Reynerie, is very ill, and as he can't have left the island, no doubt he'll be found to attend upon her; but I must say goodbye once more, Susanne. (*Aside*) I shall see you again this evening. Come along, Jacques.

JACQUES (*sorrowfully*): Goodbye all. (*Looking at* SUSANNE) Heigho! (*Exits at the door*)

HANNIBAL: That Briquet's a greater puppy than ever; and as for the other, why he's a perfect idiot. Come hustle about, it's near dinner time.

SUSANNE: Puppy, indeed! I'm sure Briquet's not at all a puppy.

LIZETTE: Nor poor Jacques half such a fool as he looks to be; but nobody is good enough for you. HANNIBAL: Yes, you're good enough for me, but don't dare dispute with me; I'll teach you to mutiny; to the right about, march!

(*They go off, he follows, right*)

Act I

Scene II

FABIAN'S HUT, *constructed of bamboo, an opening right, facing the audience, and leading to a garden. In the garden is seen a green bank, another opening at the back, which is the entrance to the hut, from which wild rocky scenery is visible. Second- entrance, left, a door leading to the interior of the hut; at the back, right, of the entrance, a small trunk, a hatchet hanging on a nail just over it. Rude couch, covered with tiger skin—a few wooden chairs left, and facing the audience. As scene opens,* CHRISTIAN, *an old Negro, is seen watching at the entrance as if looking for someone*

CHRISTIAN: How long he stays! Well, I must prepare his meal, though I fear he will not taste it. (*Looking out*) Ah! He comes at last; how unhappy he looks; when he's that way, my presence here seems to oppress him; so I'll retire, and wait till he calls me. (*Exit, left*)

(*Enter* FABIAN, *slowly, right, holding in his hand a little cross of gold, hanging from his neck; places his hat on the little trunk, and his gun near the entrance*)

FABIAN: Sacred relic, worn by my mother, and which, after I had closed her eyes in death, I took from her cold breast—when evil thoughts cross me, I press you to my lips, and all my anger is absorbed in tears. Can this little relic, so powerful against evil, avail nothing to my sufferings? In vain I place it on my burning heart; it cannot quench the passion that consumes it. To it alone I breathe my fearful secret; that I, a mulatto, and late a slave, dare to love the daughter of a white man—the daughter of him who was my master! It is madness—madness! (*falls on his knees, his hand on the foot of the cough*) Pray for me, my mother!

(CHRISTIAN *appears at the entrance, looks in, and signs to* PAULINE *to enter. She enters with* LIA, *who is leaning on her arm, and appears ill; places her on a seat near the entrance, and comes down alone*)

PAULINE (*after an effort to speak*): Monsieur Fabian.

FABIAN (*quickly turning at the sound of her voice*): Heavens! (*Rises*)

PAULINE (*advancing*): Monsieur Fabian!

FABIAN: Is it indeed you, mademoiselle, and here?

PAULINE (*with great gentleness*): When death threatened, you came to my assistance; when life and health returned, you left me; but you did not impose on me forgetfulness nor ingratitude. (*Offers a purse*)

FABIAN (*with emotion*): And it is for this you are here? Oh, mademoiselle, I thought you were good—generous—

PAULINE: The gold I have brought you, I wish you to distribute among your poor patients—

FABIAN (*taking the purse*): You are an angel. (*Looking at* LIA *with happiness*) I bless heaven for seconding my endeavors; again I see you, whom death has twice so nearly snatched away—I am happy, I am proud!

PAULINE Good Fabian! But this mystery that cause me to—

FABIAN: Mystery!

PAULINE: Yes, which perhaps you can help me to unravel. Since you have ceased to come to the Reynerie, a man has been seen at night wandering about the dwelling, near my window; he has eluded all search—all pursuit; one night the negro on duty fired at him quite at random, and next morning, at the foot of a large tree, traces of blood were found. Fabian, I cannot tell you my feelings at the sight of that blood. (*Looking earnestly at him*) You had not always that scar on your forehead.

FABIAN: That scar? A fall I had on the rock.

PAULINE (*aside, agonized*): 'Twas his blood!

FABIAN: Mademoiselle, what is the matter?

PAULINE: Fabian, the desire to thank you was not the only motive that brought me here; I have come to claim your assistance for my poor foster sister, Lia.

FABIAN: Lia! Once so happy and so gay!

PAULINE: But now so ill, so spirit-broken! Yes, Fabian, poor Lia is sinking beneath sorrows I am ignorant of; she will die if you do not save her. (*Brings Lia forward*) Look at her. Courage, dear Lia; he restored me, and will give you health and strength.

FABIAN (*gives her a seat, takes her hand, and looks at her*): What is the matter, Lia?

LIA (*without raising her head*): Nothing.

PAULINE: Dear Lia, tell Fabian the cause of your suffering.

LIA: I do not suffer.

PAULINE (*to* FABIAN): Always the same answer; you cannot assist, if she persists in the silence; she will die, and none will ever know the grief that killed her.

FABIAN: Yes, I know it.

LIA (*alarmed*): Heavens!

FABIAN: I know her malady, but cannot save her.

PAULINE (*alarmed*): What do you say?

FABIAN: The sickness that oppresses her is of the heart.

LIA (*rising in terror*): Fabian, Fabian! Oh, be silent. (*Falls back in her seat*)

PAULINE (*aside*): This mystery!

FABIAN: You love.

LIA: Oh, no, no, no, no, no.

FABIAN: Do not try to deceive me; the budding passion which brightened to your eyes during your mistress's convalescence, since then I see has grown, and consumed the heart in which you strived to stifle it.

LIA (*hiding her face in her hand*): Have pity, Fabian, have pity!

FABIAN: And this love, pure and chaste, you would hide from all, as if it were a shame for you to love one whom you have no right to love, and who despises you.

PAULINE: Oh no! 'Tis impossible.

FABIAN: Because he is not of your accursed race; because he is a European.

PAULINE: What do I hear?

FABIAN: And yet is Monsieur Bertrand a good and worthy young man.

LIA: Do not mention that name.

PAULINE: Bertrand, the young Frenchman? Mr. Barbantine's clerk?

FABIAN: Yes, mademoiselle, yes! He is a good and worthy young man; but his skin is white (*to* LIA) and yours is dark, as mine; therefore you have not the right to love him. Suffer, poor sister, suffer and despair, for yours is a malady for which there is no remedy.

PAULINE: Oh, heavens! Ought I to understand?

LIA (*weeping*): I wish to die; 'tis all I desire.

PAULINE: Unhappy girl, but you must not, shall not; I will save you. (*Looking at* FABIAN) You say he is not of her race; what is that to me, since she loves him—would die for him? You hear me, Fabian; I say she shall live, she shall be his wife.

LIA (*joyfully*): His wife!

FABIAN (*astonished*): 'Tis impossible.

PAULINE: It shall be my work, my secret care, known only to us three; he loves you?

LIA: But if he marries me, he is lost.

FABIAN: Yes, he will be proscribed, driven out by the man who has fostered him.

PAULINE: No matter, I am rich; I know it now, and for the first time feel proud of it. He shall be free, and you shall be happy. (*Looking at* FABIAN) I know not what gives me strength and resolution, before unknown to me; by-and-by we will go to Barbantine's residence; I will see Bertrand, he shall hear me, he will understand; but you, Lia, weak and suffering, must not go with me, and I will not confide our secret to another; (*with firmness*) I will go alone.

FABIAN (*sorrowfully*): Alone!

PAULINE (*with gentleness*): No, Fabian, you shall go with me; when it strikes three at St. Louis, be at the end of the avenue of palms. Come, Lia, my sister, look cheerfully, all will be well. Look, Fabian, she is better already; her eyes are brighter; thanks to you, she feels the blessings of hope, and hope is life. Come, Lia, come.

(*Exit hurriedly:* LIA *kisses his hand, and exits after her*)

FABIAN: He is of another race—what is that to me? She loves him—would die for him! She said so, here but now, and to me, who would die for her. Oh, mother, mother, bless you; I asked you, you prayed for me, and in an instant heaven has sent me a moment of joy—of bliss.

(*The report of a gun heard, and* ST. LUCE *calling without*)

ST. LUCE (*without*): Help! Help!

(CHRISTIAN *appears at the entrance, and points, left*)

CHRISTIAN: Master! Master! Yonder a hunter! A Serpent! (*Takes down hatchet, is going*)

FABIAN: You are not strong enough; give me the weapon. (*Takes hatchet from him, and rushes out*)

CHRISTIAN (*following to entrance*): No, master, no, let me go; my life is worthless, but your—

(*Enter* ST. LUCE, *conducted by* FABIAN) Ha, he was in time.

FABIAN (*to* ST. LUCE): Lean on me, sir.

ST. LUCE (*a gun in his hand*): No thank you, Doctor; I am not much hurt.

(CHRISTIAN *takes* ST. LUCE'S *hat and gun and places them in a corner*)

FABIAN (*gives hatchet to* CHRISTIAN, *who replaces it*): Some water.

(*Exit* CHRISTIAN. FABIAN *gives* ST. LUCE *a seat*)

ST. LUCE: I have many times seen death as near, but have never been on such intimate terms with a serpent before; 'tis an indigenous produce which does little honor to your country. (CHRISTIAN *returns with coconut shell full of water and gives it to* FABIAN, *who hands it to* ST. LUCE)

ST. LUCE (*returns it to* FABIAN *after drinking*): Thank you.

FABIAN (*looking at his left hand*): You are wounded.

ST. LUCE: O, 'tis nothing.

FABIAN: Allow me. (*Taking from the little trunk the necessaries to dress the wound*) What could bring you to this isolated spot?

(*Exit* CHRISTIAN, *who returns immediately with more water;* FABIAN *washes and dresses* ST. LUCE'S *wounded hand*)

ST. LUCE: Only curiosity! You must know I was stretched out under a banana tree, enjoying that dreamy repose, which, while it transports us to an ideal world, still allows us to hear what is passing in this. I dreamt I was hunting at Marly, when suddenly the foliage near me became agitated, and thinking it was a rabbit, I seized my gun, and fired, as near as I could judge, upon the spot of his hiding place, when all of a sudden I saw the grey head of an enormous serpent rise up before me; so I called out lustily for help, and my kind stars sent you to my assistance, when there was no more space between me and my enemy than just enough for your hatchet. By my faith, Doctor, you are a wonderful man, and your exact manner of amputation is complete.

FABIAN: Sir, if you ever seek rest, this miserable dwelling is at your service; but if you desire to return to St. Louis, allow me to offer a guide.

ST. LUCE (*rising*): A thousand thanks for your proffered hospitality; but I must not give my sister time to be uneasy at my absence; therefore, will only accept the guide you offer.

FABIAN (*to* CHRISTIAN): Prepare to conduct the Chevalier by the road through St. Hane.

ST. LUCE: Doctor, you are decidedly the good genius of our family; without your assistance, lovely eyes might this night have been drowned in tears; yes, my cousin would again have hid her sweet face in the grief of mourning, which is soon to smile on her affianced husband.

FABIAN (*at the back of the stage, turns suddenly round*): Affianced husband: of whom do you speak?

ST. LUCE: Of my cousin, who is to—

FABIAN: Of Mademoiselle de la Reynerie?

ST. LUCE: Certainly.

FABIAN: No, it is impossible.

ST. LUCE: Impossible: and why?

FABIAN (*embarrassed*): Because I know no one in Bourbon worthy to possess such a treasure.

ST. LUCE: True; but then I do not belong to the Isle.

FABIAN: You!

ST. LUCE: Yes, I am in love, my dear sir—seriously in love; you are astonished to hear it, they would not believe it at Versailles; but I repeat it, I'm in love, and intend to marry; our union was first projected by Madame de la Reynerie, and Pauline but waited the end of her mourning, in order to obey her mother's wish.

FABIAN (*overpowered*): She!

ST. LUCE: And though the aristocracy of Bourbon should blame me ever so, I shall insist on your presence at my marriage, which, but for you, death had twice prevented. Farewell, Doctor, or rather, goodbye for the present. (*To* CHRISTIAN, *who is standing at the entrance, and presents Chevalier with hat and gun*) Go on before me friend, and heaven protect us from sun and serpents. Goodbye, Fabian.

(*Exit* ST. LUCE *and* CHRISTIAN)

FABIAN (*with a sudden burst*): She loves that man, he will be her husband! And yet but now I have saved him! I have allowed him to go from me with life. (*Seizes his gun, is about to rush out, and suddenly stops*) Kill him! Assassinate him! No, no, 'tis not he who should die! It is, ah—I; water! Air! I shall suffocate! (*Falls at the end of the couch, his hand falls on his chest, he seizes the little cross suspended round his neck*) Again that dreadful idea crossed my brain, and my hand unintentionally falls on this little relic—O, my mother, 'tis your voice I hear, 'tis heaven commands I should avoid a crime, and still drag on this wretched life of suffering!

(*Three o'clock strikes*)

FABIAN: Three o'clock; she is waiting for me—she, St. Luce's bride! (*Rises with a sudden burst*) No, no, it shall not be! I will not die alone. (*Throws away cross*) Mother, I hear you not, you shall not save her—together, together, we will die together!

(*Rushes out*)

Act I

Scene III

The High Road near Reynerie. Enter Briquet *and* Jacques, *right; they are both a little elevated*

Pierre: Capital stuff that, wasn't it, Jacques? That's the house to live in! Long life to the Chevalier and his intended bride. I say, Jacques, my boy, why don't you laugh?

Jacques: I can't laugh, Briquet: I'm melancholy.

Pierre: It's a professional failing; tailors are naturally melancholy; sedentary employment produces thoughts, therefore it's natural.

Jacques: You've called me a natural three times.

Pierre: Don't interrupt me Jacques, but listen,—what was I saying? O, I remember; long life to the Chevalier and his intended bride! Talking of brides I intend to be married myself shortly.

Jacques: You be married! And pray who is to be the bride?

Pierre: Who's to be the bride? Why, whom do you think but Susanne, the lovely charming little Susanne?

Jacques: Have you got her consent?

Pierre: Not yet.

Jacques: Have you got her father's consent?

Pierre: Not exactly, but I've got the consent of one party.

Jacques: What, her mother?

Pierre: No (*hiccup*) myself.

Jacques: Well, that's something towards it, but I should like to see you propose it to old Grimaud, he'd—

Pierre: What do I care about old Grimaud? Do you think I'm afraid of old Grimaud? I'm afraid of nobody, when my blood's up. I fear neither man nor—(*turning round*) the devil!

(*Enter* Christian, *the old negro, right*)

Christian: Your master waits for you at the Reynerie.

Pierre: What do you know about my master?

Christian: But little! I have just acted as his guide—he met with a slight accident in the woods.

PIERRE: An accident?

CHRISTIAN: Yes, which delayed him beyond the time appointed to his return. But all danger is past, thanks to the timely assistance of my master.

PIERRE: And who is your master?

CHRISTIAN: The Black Doctor.

(*Exit, right*)

PIERRE (*turns from him as he speaks*): I say, Jacques, (*looks round, finds* CHRISTIAN *gone*) Why, he's gone; so the Black Doctor's come to hand at last. I was going down to Grimaud's, but as my new master wants me I can't, so do you tell him. Do you hear that the Black Doctor's still in the land of the living? None of your nonsense now with Susanne. I feel rather queer, but the Chevalier will attribute that to my anxiety on his account. Goodbye Jacques; keep steady, my boy; I shall see you tomorrow; keep steady—and keep me always in your eyes as an example.

(*They exit differently*)

Act I

Scene IV

Enormous rocks, left. A rock, right forming a grotto; near which, on one side is a stone bench, a rock in which steps are rudely cut, descending to the sea in the center of the stage; with a rock in which a seat appears rudely cut. A pathway, left, a little elevated, and overhanging the steep cliffs. The whole scene is wild and gloomy in the extreme; the sea at back. As the scene opens PAULINE and FABIAN appears at the very top of the rock, right

PAULINE: This path seems unfrequented; why have we come this way?

FABIAN: The inhabitants rarely visit this bay, which they have called the mulatto's grotto; there is a popular legend attached to it.

PAULINE: Shall we reach the Reynerie before Bertrand? I wish to be first, to tell Lia of the success of our enterprise.

FABIAN: He is going round in the boat; the wind and tide will be against him, so we have the advantage. Rest yourself here a moment to recruit your strength.

PAULINE (*sits on rock, center of stage*): This is a wild and gloomy spot.

FABIAN: Did you not desire me to take the most retired route? Mademoiselle de la Reynerie wished to avoid anyone whilst walking beside the mulatto Fabian. 'Twas otherwise in your childhood; then you did not disdain to lean on my arm.

PAULINE (*after a moment's silence as if to change the conversation*): Fabian, I think you have my fan.

FABIAN (*takes it from his bosom, and presents it to her respectfully*): 'Tis here, Mademoiselle.

PAULINE: But, you too must be tired, Fabian, for your hand trembles so as it did just now; are you ill?

FABIAN: No, lady.

PAULINE: Ah, I shall be so happy to tell Lia the obstacles that separated her from Bertrand no longer exist; in a month she shall leave the colony with her affianced husband; they shall live in a country where prejudice will not condemn their union—will not crush their mutual affection; Lia, my sister you at least shall be happy. (*Sighing*)

FABIAN: Happy! Yes, in the love of her husband! For without his love of what avail would have been my penetration or your generous friendship?

PAULINE: Bertrand has a noble heart.

FABIAN: He loves her.

PAULINE: He was not born under your sky; had he been a creole, he would have hid his passion in the utmost depths of his heart.

FABIAN: And Lia would have perished; and had Bertrand been a creole he dared not have shed one tear to her memory; is it not so?

PAULINE (*rising with calm dignity*): Fabian, we will continue our walk; the Countess and her brother will be waiting for me.

FABIAN (*endeavoring to contain himself*): He loves you, lady.

PAULINE (*embarrassed*): He has told me so.

FABIAN: He is to be your husband.

PAULINE: 'Twas my mother's dearest wish. (FABIAN *staggers against the rock, right;* PAULINE *is going, turns round and looks at him*) Fabian, I am waiting for you.

(*He passes his hand across his forehead, appears to be looking attentively at two crosses carved in one of the rocks*)

FABIAN: Those two crosses carved in the rock, and which appertain to the legend I told you of just now.

PAULINE: What legend?

FABIAN: Shall tell you?

PAULINE: Yes, tell me the history of this legend.

FABIAN (*goes back, looks at the sea which is seen gradually to rise, then returns to* PAULINE): Listen, then. There lived in St. Louis, a poor mulatto—a slave, who (I have forgotten for what good service rendered to his master) received his freedom! The generous gift should have made him happy, but it was otherwise; for once free he was compelled to leave his master's dwelling, and under that roof dwelt his better angel. At length he went forth, more wretched in his freedom than in his slavery! For he loved—yes madly loved—adored that master's daughter.

(*Wind heard*)

PAULINE (*alarmed*): How dreadfully the wind howls.

FABIAN (*not heeding her*): He would have buried his love in his heart, though it had crushed it; but the young and noble lady, who used to converse with him, in few kind words, completed the delusion. He thought himself beloved—and though respect to the pride of her race forbade her to be his, he thought at least she would never be another's. The fool was dreaming; one word awoke him, she was about to marry—to marry! She had deceived him, had sported with his agony; she should not have done so—it was imprudent for then the wretched man took an oath to unite himself to her by the solemn, dreadful, awful tie of death.

PAULINE (*rising agitated, looks at the sea, which is gradually surrounding them*): Fabian! Fabian! Not now; the sea rises. (*Going*) Let us go. Come, come, Fabian!

FABIAN: (*detains her*) Go! (*Smiles*) No, the mulatto had calculated every chance; in his turn he had deceived the young girl—he had led her into a snare—they both stood here—on the spot we now occupy; the tide was rising fast, only one path was free—but the sea continued to gain on them. (*Seizes both her hands*) The young girl entreated the mulatto to try to save her; but he, without pity for her terror or her tears, held her with hands of iron. At last he told her he loved her. (*Looking round*) Still the sea was gaining ground; every chance of escape was gone, and yet death has less of horror for the young girl than the mulatto's love.

PAULINE (*in much terror*): Fabian, for pity's sake, save me!

FABIAN: Save you! And is it not possible you guess I love you?

PAULINE (*struggling with her feelings*): No, no! You are deceiving me; you would not—could not see me die here before your eyes!

FABIAN (*pointing to sea*): Look, Pauline, before we should reach the rocks which we now but descended together, the sea would dash us to atoms against their rugged points! I feared my own weakness, and closed every avenue to the road of repentance or pity; death surrounds us, but we shall perish together! How! You no longer tremble, will you not call down heaven's curses on your destroyer's head?

PAULINE (*solemnly*): Fabian!

FABIAN (*pointing to sea*): No earthly power can save us!

PAULINE (*rushing to pathway, which the sea has not yet reached*)
Then let me beg my mother's forgiveness and pray to heaven
for you. (*Falls on her knees against the rock*)

FABIAN: For me!

PAULINE: Yes, for you! Now I am sure of death, I may acknowledge,
without shame or remorse, that I understand you, Fabian,
and I forgive you, for I have long, long loved you!

FABIAN: Did I hear aright? Love me! And I—I am her murderer!
Oh, heavens, (*rushes to her and supports her in his arms*) you
will not allow it! Kill me! But save her! (*Looks around*) Ah!
'Tis too late! She is already dying. (*Carries her up the rock, lays
her down, takes off his vest, waves it, shouting for help. The sea
reaches them, curtain falls as he is still struggling with her in the
water.* BERTRAND *is seen at the back in a boat*)

Curtain.

Act II

A handsome drawing room in the MARCHIONESS's *Home in Paris, elegantly furnished. At the back, large folding doors, opening to a gallery; on each side, at the back, a large window, with hangings, a door left and right; handsome bookcase and bureau on each side; canopy, left, armchairs right and left—a handbell on the bookcase. Enter* BRIQUET *and* JACQUES, *very handsomely and foppishly dressed, and rather grotesquely*

PIERRE: And so, friend Jacques, you have followed us to Paris?

JACQUES: Yes, I felt so dull when you left, that I made up my mind to come too; but what a grand house to be sure!

PIERRE (*offers snuff*): Yes, we are pleasantly situated. Do you still operate?

(*Makes sign of cutting with shears*)

JACQUES: Yes, I cut out.

PIERRE: Ah, you rogue, you have cut me out; and how does Madame Fils?

JACQUES: Oh, she's quite well.

PIERRE: Delighted to hear it—shall be still more delighted to see her. I bear no ill-will; but how the deuce you managed it, I never could guess.

JACQUES: Why, you see, I didn't talk of marrying until I got more than my own consent in the business.

PIERRE: Ha, ha, I recollect; but really, in Paris, a wife is rather an incumbrance, and you see my situation brings me so much in contact with the fashionable world, that one don't miss the little comforts, as they are termed, of matrimony; strange things have happened since we rusticated in St. Louis.

JACQUES: Strange, indeed, to think that the Marchioness, whom we all supposed drowned, should be alive after all.

PIERRE: Yes, and she is gone to Versailles, to present her daughter, Madame Pauline, to her Majesty, the Queen, upon her return from the colonies; she'll be back in an hour.

JACQUES: And the Black Doctor?

PIERRE: Oh, he's with us—couldn't do without him; though, by-the-by, the Marchioness doesn't much relish his being here; but the circumstance of his having twice saved her daughter's life, and her still delicate health, in some way reconcile her to his presence.

JACQUES: That was a fearful business, too, when Monsieur Bertrand saved them both; there was a sort of mystery in that affair!

PIERRE: No doubt, no doubt, friend Jacques; there are more mysteries than we can fathom in this world; it was, as you say, a close shave.

JACQUES: Rather too fine-drawn an affair for me, I own; and the marriage with the Chevalier!

PIERRE: Why, there seems some reluctance on her part, but the Marchioness is positive. I suppose, eventually, she must marry; but come into my room, and we will take a glass to old times, and our future acquaintance.

(*As they are going, enter* ANDRE *at the door in back, which is open*)

PIERRE: And what do you want, friend?

ANDRE: The Doctor, if you please.

PIERRE: This is not a doctor's shop, friend; you are in the house of the Marchioness de la Reynerie.

ANDRE: Yes, I know; but he I seek lives here.

PIERRE: Who is it you mean?

ANDRE: The Doctor; the good worthy man I have come to thank; he's well-known in our quarter, ever since he attended my poor mother; everybody gave her up, even the hospital doctors; and today, thanks to him, she's quite well again! Oh, he's got plenty of practice; but he always gives the poor the preference; and when he passes our way, men, women, and children bless the Black Doctor.

PIERRE: The Black Doctor! Oh, now I know who you mean. He means Fabian.

ANDRE: Is that his name?

PIERRE: Yes, he's a mulatto, an enfranchised slave, whom Mademoiselle de la Reynerie brought over from Bourbon, a curiosity.

(FABIAN *appears at door, dressed in court suit, sword, etc.*)

ANDRE: A curiosity, indeed! Goodness and charity are, no doubt, a curiosity to you; take care how you speak about him before me!

FABIAN (*comes down*): Noble heart!

ANDRE: Ah, is that you, Doctor?

PIERRE: Come along, Jacques.

ANDRE: Why, Doctor, how dares that powdered monkey—

FABIAN (*calmly*): How is your mother, today, Andre?

ANDRE: Well, quite well; she sent me, though strong enough to come herself, but she was afraid—

FABIAN: Afraid!

ANDRE: This is how it is, Doctor; we took it into our heads that, as everybody must live by their trade, a doctor can't give away his time to everybody for nothing; so I worked double tides, and have brought you a fortnight's wages; it isn't much, but such as it is there it is.

FABIAN: I accept your offer, good friend, but you must be my banker, and when you meet with a fellow-creature who needs it more than yourself, give it to him.

ANDRE: From you?

FABIAN: As you please.

ANDRE: I'll do as you desire! Farewell, Mr. Fabian; don't forget Andre. In a few months I am going to my brother in Bretagne—'tis our country.

FABIAN: Bretagne?

ANDRE: Yes, if you should ever come there you shall have the best place at our fireside, as you already have in our hearts. Farewell, Mr. Fabian. (*Exit at door, first shaking* FABIAN's *hand*)

FABIAN (*seats himself, and finishes reading a letter, which he has in his hand*): "Yes, Fabian, with Bertrand, my husband, who loves me more than ever, in the bosom of his family, who welcomed me as another child; I am happy, very happy; when you hear of this, ah, let us hear of your happiness, too." (*refolds the letter ironically*) Happy! Yes, my good Lia, I live in a noble house, am head lackey to the Marchioness de la Reynerie— distinguished honor! True, I am waited on by my fellow servants, in my own apartment. Oh, yes, I am happy, very happy! (*Rising*) Heavens! Whence comes this patience, this resignation? For six long months have I endured this, and yet I have not roused my sleeping energies, and cried aloud to them all. She whom you surround with such homage, such flattery, she is mine, my own, my wife! No, I am silent. Shut up the livelong day, I endeavor to forget my condition in study, and only when I hear the carriage which conveys the Marchioness from the door, do I venture to exchange a look—a word with Pauline, then a stranger comes, and I must needs retire, a smile and a tear—(*Noise of carriage, he runs to window and looks out*) 'Tis she! I shall see her, I shall see her. Oh, this is the secret of my resignation.

(*A servant opens the folding doors, the Chevalier, in court dress enters, conducting* PAULINE, *who is also in court dress.* ST. LUCE *does not notice* FABIAN, *who stands aside, and is not seen by* PAULINE. *Aside*)

FABIAN: Still that man forever at her side!

ST. LUCE: Now, cousin! Cannot the gracious reception you met with at Versailles, raise a smile in that beautiful face? For my part, like the Marchioness, I was delighted as I observed the looks of our charming Queen wander from yourself to rest on me—she doubtless guessed what I could poorly conceal.

PAULINE: Your pardon, Chevalier, my mother, I believe, is waiting for you.

ST. LUCE: May I not be excused for forgetting her, when by your side? (*Aside*) Ever cold and constrained! I cannot understand it. Adieu, for the present my lovely cousin! Do try to think a little of me until I see you again, I shall think of no one else.

(*He is about to kiss her hand, she withdraws it, he signifies his mortification; as he is going, stops on seeing* FABIAN)

ST. LUCE: So, you were here, were you?

PAULINE (*surprised*): Fabian!

ST. LUCE: In the drawing room, we may readily discern we are not in Bourbon, and are making rapid strides towards equality, as the commons have it. (*Aside*) This is very strange, but doubtless you have come for mademoiselle's order—you should have knocked sir. If there are no longer slaves in Paris, I believe we still have lackeys.

(*Exit at door*)

FABIAN: True, a slave in Bourbon! Here a lackey.

PAULINE (*in a supplicating voice*): But the slave! The lackey! Is he not my lord—my husband in the sight of heaven, and in mine, who lives for him? Is he not great, is he not noble, has he not a right to be proud of himself? Do you not bear next your heart a sacred deed, signed by a minister of heaven—a deed that plainly says "That the lackey—the slave—is my master?"

IRA ALDRIDGE

FABIAN: Our marriage, blessed by an unknown minister, in an isolated corner in the Isle of Bourbon, your mother will have power to break, by a simple motion of her fan. (*Drawing a paper from his breast*) Since this may not be the passport of business for either, at least it can be made the instrument of revenge.

PAULINE (*calmly*): Yes, Fabian, you can show it to my mother; you can say to her, your daughter has changed her proud name of La Reynerie for that of Fabian; your daughter has even given herself to me. You can do all this, and I should forgive you; but my mother would curse the memory of her child!

FABIAN: Oh, forgive me, Pauline, forgive me; you know not what I suffer, you know not my wretchedness; but fear not, I will bear up against the grief that is killing me, against the jealousy that consumes me.

PAULINE What, Fabian, jealousy?

FABIAN: No, no doubt ever entered my heart, it would kill me at once. Pauline, I will be confiding, calm! I shall see you daily go to those fetes where so many temptations surround you, but I will be silent; you will accept his arm for your escort, that man who is ever at your side, that man who loves you, I shall see him, as I did but now, gaze on you with admiration, raise that hand to his lips, which is mine—I say, I shall see all this, and yet I shall be silent.

MARCHIONESS DE LA REYNERIE (*without*): Pauline, 'tis I, open the door.

PAULINE: My mother, and she will find me here, and with you.

FABIAN (*rushes to window*): No, though I should be dashed to atoms on the pavement below.

PAULINE: Stay! (*Pointing to the chamber*) There, in that room, by the back staircase, hasten.

MARCHIONESS DE LA REYNERIE (*without*): Pauline! Pauline, I say!

FABIAN (*going by direction, right*): You see I am obedient. I am going; I shall be silent.

(*Exit* FABIAN. *Enter the* MARCHIONESS, *center*)

MARCHIONESS DE LA REYNERIE (*looking round*): Were you alone, Pauline?

PAULINE (*embarrassed*): Yes, yes, mother, alone.

MARCHIONESS DE LA REYNERIE: When the Chevalier left you, Fabian was here.

PAULINE: He was.

MARCHIONESS DE LA REYNERIE: How did the man presume to enter here, without your express order?

PAULINE (*hesitating*): He came to tell me of a visit he had paid to some poor pensioners of mine, as I had desired him.

MARCHIONESS DE LA REYNERIE (*haughtily*): And I desire you may have no such explanations in the future; tomorrow he shall leave this house, and in three days quit France.

PAULINE: He! Fabian?

MARCHIONESS DE LA REYNERIE: I am about to send him back to the colony, there he will henceforth enjoy independence. I will reward him, as I ought, for his faithful servitude to you; but let us speak no more of the man, but come at once to the business that brings me here now. The Queen was pleased with you, my daughter, and in order to have you one of her ladies of honor, her Majesty wishes you to marry.

PAULINE: What do I hear?

MARCHIONESS DE LA REYNERIE: The Chevalier St. Luce will this evening receive letters patent that will confer on him the title of Count, and tomorrow the King will add to the obligations I already owe him, by himself signing your contract.

PAULINE: No, no, I did not hear aright; mother, 'tis impossible!

MARCHIONESS DE LA REYNERIE: Impossible! Listen to me, Pauline; I have determined to have you a noble protector, and a defender; I could not confide my child to one more noble or more worthy than St. Luce, already almost my son. I repeat, 'tis my determination you should marry him, and by the memory of your father, it shall be as I say.

(*Goes to bookcase and rings bell*)

PAULINE (*aside*): Then 'tis heaven's will I should die!

(*Enter servant, center*)

MARCHIONESS DE LA REYNERIE: Tell Fabian I have an important command for him; show all visitors into this apartment, I will receive him here.

(*Exit servant*)

MARCHIONESS DE LA REYNERIE (*To* PAULINE): You will for the future receive the Chevalier as your intended husband.

(Pauline *knees to her, kisses her hand, and weeps*) Pauline, you cannot make me alter my determination! Your resistance would be as useless as your prayers.

PAULINE: Mother, heaven is my witness, I would have devoted to you the life you gave me. I asked, I sought, but to live in your heart, and you drive me from you!

MARCHIONESS DE LA REYNERIE: To give you to the arms of a husband.

PAULINE: Before your will excludes me and separates us, my mother, gaze on me as you used to do; when a child I looked for and found all, all my joys in your eyes; bless me as you used to do, when I prayed to heaven that I might live and die for my mother's love.

MARCHIONESS DE LA REYNERIE (*raising her*): Tomorrow, Pauline, at the altar, I will bless both my children.

PAULINE (*aside*) Tomorrow you will have no daughter!

(*Servant opens door at back*)

MARCHIONESS DE LA REYNERIE: Calm yourself, Pauline; we are no longer alone.

(*Servant announces the following ladies and gentlemen: Countess* DE RESADEUC, MDLLE. *and* CHEVALIER DE ST. LUCE, MADAME DE BEAUOMEAL, MONSIEUR *and* MADAME DE LA FRERAGE, MARCHIONESS L'AMBERVILLE, *Councillor Ommissor. All the company is received by the* MARCHIONESS, *who presents them to* PAULINE *as they enter; she curtsies to them all; the* MARCHIONESS *conducts the ladies to the canopy, and places herself in an armchair beside it;* PAULINE, *struggling with emotion, conducts one of the ladies right; one chair remains unoccupied between her and the lady; the gentlemen remain standing in groups behind the ladies right and left; the Countess* DE RESADEUC *alone remains standing for a moment by the* MARCHIONESS)

AURELIA: My good aunt, at length the dearest wish of my heart will be fulfilled. St. Luce has just told me—

MARCHIONESS DE LA REYNERIE (*smiling*): That I am a very humble and obedient subject. It is my intention it should be known at Versailles this very evening, that I have presented the Countess de St. Luce, lady of honor to her Majesty, the Queen, to all my friends.

ALL: Lady of honor!

(The gentlemen compliment St. Luce*)*

Aurelia: At length, then you are my sister. *(Taking* Pauline's *hand)*

Pauline *(aside)*: Heaven! Give me one hour more of strength and courage!

St. Luce: My dear aunt, I know not how to thank you; but believe me, I will prove worthy of the treasure you confide to me. *(kisses the hand of* Reynerie, *approaches* Pauline, *who remains motionless)* How! Not one look?

(Enter Servant, center)

Servant: Monsieur Fabian, Madam.

Pauline: Fabian!

St. Luce: She starts at the name!

Marchioness De La Reynerie: Very well, tell him to wait.

Aurelia *(to* Marchioness de la Reynerie*)*: Poor Fabian, I have scarcely seen him since his arrival, and I have talked so much about him to these ladies that they are as anxious to see him as I was at the Isle of Bourbon.

Marchioness De La Reynerie: In this apartment! You forget.

Aurelia *(laughing)*: O, they won't know of it in Bourbon.

Pauline *(aside)*: Before so many he will betray himself.

St. Luce *(aside)*: Pale, trembling. 'Twas the same this morning, and always so at the question of his name! By heaven! I will know how far she is interested in this man. My dear aunt, allow me to join in my sister's entreaty; besides, I owe Fabian a debt.

Marchioness De La Reynerie: You!

St. Luce: Yes, of honor.

Marchioness De La Reynerie: Well, dear Count, today I cannot refuse you anything. *(To servant)* Tell Fabian he may come in.

(Exit servant)

Pauline *(aside)*: We are lost!

St. Luce *(laughing)*: Quite a presentation, I declare.

(Enter Fabian. At sight of company he stops; upon a sign from the Marchioness *bows and addresses her)*

Fabian: You sent for me, madam; what are your commands?

Aurelia *(to a lady)*: What do you think of him?

Marchioness De La Reynerie: You are about to quit my house to leave France.

AURELIA: Why? Where is he going?

MARCHIONESS DE LA REYNERIE: To Bourbon.

FABIAN (*quickly*): Madam, I—(*Catches* PAULINE's *eye, stops*)

ST. LUCE (*Aside*): How she watches him!

FABIAN: When am I to depart, madam?

MARCHIONESS DE LA REYNERIE: Tomorrow; the steward has received my orders. You will find that I have not forgotten past services, nor been unmindful of your future welfare; you may now retire.

ST. LUCE (*to* MARCHIONESS): Not yet, my dear aunt; you must allow me to beg you will delay his departure for a few days. Fabian, we are no longer at Bourbon; therefore I can and will reward you for the service you there rendered me; the invitation I there gave you I hold good here, and repeat, I wish you to be present at my marriage with Mademoiselle de la Reynerie, (*looks from* FABIAN *to* PAULINE) which will be celebrated in three days.

(FABIAN *suddenly starts.* PAULINE *instantly rises, and takes her eyes from him.* FABIAN, *struggling with his feelings, endeavours to be calm and silent. Aside*)

ST. LUCE: Again! At all hazard I will know the worst.

AURELIA: You will grant my brother's request, will you not, dear aunt? Fabian, you do not thank my brother.

ST. LUCE (*smiles contemptuously*): No, I remember; 'tis very natural; he does not like to own himself so bad a prophet. Fabian has declared all marriage impossible for Mademoiselle de la Reynerie.

MARCHIONESS DE LA REYNERIE: He!

ST. LUCE: Yes, my dear aunt; doubtless he was afraid of losing so profitable and unexpected a source of patronage and favor. (*Looks at* PAULINE) What other motive could there be? I am afraid our cousin's protection has been thoughtless, and perhaps may be fatal to our Doctor.

MARCHIONESS DE LA REYNERIE: How?

ST. LUCE: No doubt, in Bourbon 'twill be necessary to duff these trappings of a gentleman which appear rather strange; here 'tis only laughed at, but in Bourbon 'twould be otherwise; there his insolence would be chastised, particularly the sword, which sits but ill on a mulatto, who could not dare to raise it even to ward off the planter's whip!

PAULINE (*without taking her eyes from* FABIAN): Ah!

AURELIA: Brother, you are cruel!

ST. LUCE (*haughtily*) No, sister; 'tis not I, but reason that says every man in his station. Look! Fabian already pays dearly for the ridiculous dreams to which an imputed benevolence has given birth; he suffers, for he cannot forget what he was—what he is! See how he plays with the hilt of the sword! That hand, which still wears the impression of the chain—

FABIAN (*in a fury*) Ah! (Draws the sword and with a sudden expression breaks it, throws it at his feet, and covering his face with his hands, weeps)

ST. LUCE: Why, what's the matter?

AURELIA (*coming between them*): Brother, you are very cruel; you have wounded his feelings.

PAULINE (*rushing forward*): I can endure this no longer; 'tis cowardly—infamous! (*Goes to her mother and speaks in a voice choked with passion and sobs*) Mother, dismiss these people; I must speak to you alone!

MARCHIONESS DE LA REYNERIE (*rising*): This agitation!

PAULINE: Have pity on me—on yourself! Dismiss them!

MARCHIONESS DE LA REYNERIE (*aside to her*): You alarm me, Pauline! Friends, my daughter is ill; it alarms me!

AURELIA: Indeed! (*To* PAULINE) Are you ill?

MARCHIONESS DE LA REYNERIE: Leave us to ourselves! Chevaliers, adieu until tomorrow!

(*Exit guests*)

ST. LUCE (*Aside*): If you have indeed favored this unruly rival, cousin, I have at least paid your insult by insult. Come, sister.

(*Takes her hand; as he is leading her off gives a look of scorn at* FABIAN, *who is following him*)

PAULINE: No, no—stay, Fabian!

MARCHIONESS DE LA REYNERIE: Why do you detain him?

PAULINE: Because if you drive him forth, you must also drive me forth; because if he goes, 'tis my duty to follow him.

MARCHIONESS DE LA REYNERIE: To follow Fabian!

PAULINE: Yes, mother, my love—my lord—my husband!

MARCHIONESS DE LA REYNERIE: He!

PAULINE (*to him*): Look up, loved and injured Lord; heaven, that gives you resignation, has at last given me courage; can you forgive me?

MARCHIONESS DE LA REYNERIE: Fabian's wife! No, you did not say that?

PAULINE: I have said it, mother, and my husband shall not be dishonoured.

MARCHIONESS DE LA REYNERIE: Wretched girl, take then—

FABIAN (*coming between them*): Be not in such haste to curse, lady! Your malediction would be impious and could not reach to heaven. She, who now humbles herself, who weeps, is pure as the angels. True, she loved me, a poor slave—because I had staked my life to save her mother's; but I tell you your blood runs in her veins. She was ashamed of her love, and only on the brink of a precipice, death surrounding us, when help appeared impossible, as with her last breath, her secret escaped her.

MARCHIONESS DE LA REYNERIE: Heavens, was I restored to life but to be witness of this dishonor? This infamous marriage shall be dissolved.

FABIAN: Dissolve my marriage! You cannot do it, madam; call your servants—they shall make way for your daughter's husband; recall the Chevalier St. Luce, who so insolently crushed me with his aristocracy, and whom but for Pauline's imploring look, I would have annihilated as I did that weapon; call him, and I will tell my insolent rival 'tis now his turn to feel the torments of jealousy and rage, for his betrothed is my lawful wedded wife!

MARCHIONESS DE LA REYNERIE: I will invoke the judge, the magistrate, the King himself!

FABIAN: All slaves who set foot on European ground are free; therefore am I, before affranchised, now doubly so; and the law makes no distinction of rank or colony.

MARCHIONESS DE LA REYNERIE (*to* PAULINE): You hear him— you hear this man proclaim our shame! If your father could rise from his grave, he would strike you dead! He would rather see you in your grave than so degraded, so dishonored!

PAULINE (*takes a small phial from her bosom*): Then let him judge me! Father, I come!

(FABIAN *rushes to her, seizes phial, throws it away*)

FABIAN: Pauline!

MARCHIONESS DE LA REYNERIE: What does this mean?

FABIAN: It means, madam, that she was about to swallow poison.

MARCHIONESS DE LA REYNERIE: Poison!

FABIAN: Yes, which she had concealed, that your curse might fall upon her corpse!

MARCHIONESS DE LA REYNERIE (*sinking overpowered into a chair*): Pauline!

PAULINE (*kneeling*): I cannot live under my mother's malediction.

FABIAN: Then 'tis for me to complete this act of devotion. What neither your King nor your laws can do, Fabian himself will act. This marriage—consecrated by a holy minister of heaven, who will reveal the secret to no one—this inviolable—this indissoluble marriage, I myself will annul.

PAULINE: You!

MARCHIONESS DE LA REYNERIE: How say you?

FABIAN (*struggling with his grief*): Madam, I restore to you your daughter. Pauline, this one act has repaid me hours of grief and misery, and anguish; you would have died for me, you shall live for your mother! (*Forces her to* MARCHIONESS) Farewell, Pauline; you cannot be mine till we meet again in heaven! (*At the door*) Not mine, Pauline, but never another's! Farewell!

(*Exit*)

PAULINE: Mother, he leaves me but to seek comfort in death!

(*Tries to follow him.* MARCHIONESS *detains her*)

MARCHIONESS DE LA REYNERIE (*to servants, who enter*): Follow Fabian, see you do not let him leave the house. Should it be necessary, use force; but on no account let him depart.

Act III

The stage is divided horizontally in two parts, each part again divided into two portions. The portion right, above, forms a well-lighted apartment, splendidly furnished; at back, a window with curtains; left, a toilet-table, dressing-glass, center, a table with an armchair on each side; a door leading to staircase, which forms left of upper portion; at foot of staircase, a trap-door leading to dungeon below. The staircase is not seen, but forms left lower portion; lower portion, right, is the dungeon; a large stone pillar, behind which, is straw; in front of and right of pillar, a stone bench; left of pillar, at back, a window, with iron bars; on front pillar, on block of stone, a lighted lamp. BRIQUET *is discovered in the upper apartment reading a newspaper.*

PIERRE: Eleventh of July—then I have been as an inhabitant of the Royal Chateau, the Bastille, two months and six days exactly, and why? "Briquet," said my master, Monsieur de St. Luce, "you are my valet, I give you twelve hundred francs a year to wait upon me, shave me, dress me and powder my wig, in whatever corner of France I may be. The King sends me to the Bastille, therefore you must follow me, to dress, shave, and powder me, in the Bastille." (*Rises*) And here we are, lodged in the tower of the chapel, just above the moat. This apartment is not so bad, nor the bedroom either; the furniture is good, I may say, elegant; in short, 'tis a gentlemanly prison, but still it is a prison!

(*Drums without*)

PIERRE: Hallo! What does that mean? First time I've heard them since we've been here; perhaps the King's coming to see us and give us our liberty.

(*Drums again*)

(Enter ST. LUCE, in drawing gown)

ST. LUCE: Briquet! What, rascal! Didn't you hear me?

PIERRE Yes sir; did you say the carriage, sir?

ST. LUCE: Eh?

PIERRE I beg your pardon, sir; I'm always forgetting we are in "status quo."

ST. LUCE (*laughing*): We must accustom ourselves to it, Briquet. (*Sits*) Come, dress my hair.

PIERRE (*getting comb, etc.*): But sir, aren't you going to try to get out of here?

ST. LUCE (*looking in a hand mirror*): I beg pardon? Never! I've done the King great service and he has punished me! So much the worse for him.

PIERRE (*combing his hair*): And me too! I beg your pardon, but it seems to me you did—

ST. LUCE: My duty, sir! I was breakfasting at the "cafe de joie"; facing me were three citizens. I should have known the plebians a mile off, by the smell of them. They were members of the new assembly of deputies of the States General, chatting on public affairs. (*Looks in glass*) A little more powder on that side. At the mention of a proposition, which I did not approve of, I rose and addressed them, and flatly told them I thought everything of the aristocracy, very little of the clergy, and nothing of the people; so we warmed upon the subject until we quarreled. I offered to fight one of them; he accepted! "My name," said I, "is the Chevalier de St. Luce." "Sir," says the fellow, "my name is Barnaby." "Never heard of it," said I. Then the bystanders threw themselves between us, and separated Barnaby and me; but the adventure reached the ears of the court. Well, thinks I, Barnaby will be arrested; but instead of that they arrested me.

PIERRE: Yes, sir, I understand; but I never offended Barnaby, so I—

ST. LUCE: What do complain of? The lodging's well enough, the table is well served, the wine excellent, and the air of captivity a fine thing for the appetite. Ring for my dinner.

PIERRE (*taking glass from* ST. LUCE): Yes, sir, but then you didn't leave your heart at the gate of the Bastille, while I—but, perhaps I haven't told you I was just going to be married?

ST. LUCE: Oh, yes, you did; I thought it a capital joke.

PIERRE Not for my intended, though—poor little Runnette, I appointed to meet her by the third tree on the left-hand side of the park, and she's been waiting there two months and six days exactly; how impatient she must be.

ST. LUCE: Oh, don't make yourself uneasy; she's found amusements, I dare say; a great many of the national guards pass through the park.

PIERRE: Sir, don't talk in that way, or I shall be capable of setting fire to the Bastille.

ST. LUCE: Well, I won't prevent you; but first see after the dinner.

PIERRE Yes, sir, I'll get the table ready. Poor Runnette, how tired she must be.

(*Exit*)

ST. LUCE: Poor fellow! He also is jealous. My suspicion is right. Pauline loved Fabian, and must have owned it to her mother; for when I presented myself at the house I was informed he had departed for the Isle of Bourbon and would never return to France. The Marchioness had left Paris, taking Pauline with her; she was to become a nun! By my faith, to be trifled with, deceived, and sacrificed for a mulatto! I know not where to hide my shame; fortunately the King came to my assistance, and hid me and my blushes in the Bastille.

(*Drums heard*)

ST. LUCE: What the devil's the matter today? Briquet!

PIERRE: Perhaps it is some fete day.

(*Heavy bell heard*)

PIERRE: Hark to the bell of Notre Dame!

(*Both look out of window*)

(*Enter* JAILOR, *left, followed by Cook with the dinner. They place it on the table. Cook exits, and* JAILOR *locks the door*)

ST. LUCE (*at window*): Oh, here's my dinner. (*To* JAILOR) What have you brought me?

JAILOR (*Giving* BRIQUET *a basket*): Everything we could get of the best, Chevalier, and, as usual, wine from the governor's cellar.

ST. LUCE: You are a capital fellow, and full of little delicate attentions. (*Looks into basket*) What! No ice? I must have some ice, or I shall send a complaint to the King.

PIERRE: Dine without ice! Impossible!

JAILOR: It isn't our fault, sir; an express was sent off this morning to procure some, but it isn't come yet. The parks and public places are crowded with people, and every place is very difficult of access.

ST. LUCE: What's their difficulty of movement to me?

PIERRE: Certainly not, we see not so much room to move about.

(*Exit right with basket.* JAILOR *goes to window*)

ST. LUCE: They ought to have an icehouse in the place, but they have no consideration for state prisoners. By-the-by, I sent a request to the ministers; I have asked for a room where I can have better air. Can anything be more scandalous than to lodge a gentleman even with the moat, in the very cellar, for I suppose there can be nothing underneath us!

JAILOR (*at window*): No sir, nothing underneath.

ST. LUCE: What are you staring at, eh?

JAILOR (*leaving window quickly*): Me, sir!

ST. LUCE (*at window*): I am not mistaken—they are arranging cannon on the rampart, to the left.

JAILOR: Possibly.

ST. LUCE: Can these plebeians have begun their system?

(*Drum*)

ST. LUCE: Yes, that's the call to arms! By heaven, if I were but free, I could wish for nothing better than the command of a company of musketeers to sweep the path clean of these rascals!

PIERRE (*at door*): Dinner, ready, sir.

ST. LUCE: Bravo! Let but the King give these gentlemen of Paris a good lesson, and the minister send them a few leaden sugar plums, I'll forgive them both for making me dine without ice!

(*Exit. Enter Second* JAILOR *from staircase*)

SECOND JAILER: The storm threatens! They are only waiting for the cannon from the Invalides, to attack the Bastille. The governor fears the insurgents may gain some communication with the prisoners! Come, quick!

(*Exit both, left door, and lock it*)

(*The straw behind the pillar in dungeon, compartment right, is seen to move, and* FABIAN *pale and haggard, raises himself, passes his hand over his forehead, and rises with difficulty; takes the lamp, approaches window, looks out, listens, then retires discouraged; puts lamp on stone*)

FABIAN (*shaking his head*): Nothing! Still nothing! (*shivering*) The damp has penetrated my very limbs! I asked them for a little fresh straw, and they said it would cost too much! Straw! Your hatred and revenge are well obeyed here, proud Marchioness! It would have been more merciful to let me die than bury me alive. While I thought to purchase Pauline's pardon by my exile, they threw me into this tomb! Why should I complain? Death will come quicker here; but Pauline, what has become of her? (*Warms his hands over lamp*) My limbs are frozen, but here, (*places hand on heart*) here I am on fire! Kind heaven, preserve my reason till Andre's return; but why should I expect him? May not what I fancy to be recollection, be but a dream? For now I doubt everything! My memory, my thoughts, my existence; and yet, no, I remember well, yesterday I was sitting there—there, when a voice struck upon my ear, and that voice was Andre's; yes, Andre, who was at work in that gloomy gallery. I called, whispered my name, but he could not understand that the voice of a man proceeded from the bowels of the earth! (*Listens again*) Nothing! Nothing! (*Falls, overwhelmed*) Andre will not come!

(*A stone falls at this moment through the window, a letter attached to it*)

FABIAN: What's that?

(*Picks up letter*)

FABIAN: A letter from him; yes, yes, it is; thanks Andre! Thank heaven! (*Weeps, at last he opens letter*)

(*At this moment, JAILOR is seen, descending staircase; he opens trap, carries a loaf of bread and a jug of water FABIAN reads letter by lamp, while JAILOR descends into left division, below*)

FABIAN: "My dear benefactor, I know not if I shall be fortunate enough to see you; all Paris is in arms, and they are firing on all who approach the Bastille; but you shall have the letter, though they take my life." My good Andre! "I have been to the Marchioness's house, and it was filled with mourning; the hall was hung with black. (*He is almost choked with emotion*) A priest was in prayer beside an escutcheoned coffin, covered with velvet. I asked who was dead in the house, and they answered—

(*Enter JAILOR quickly; FABIAN has just time to hide the letter*)

JAILOR (*puts bread and water on stone*): Here!

FABIAN: Thank you.

JAILOR: Yesterday, while a man was at work in that gallery (*Pointing to window*) you approached that opening; the sentinel saw the light from your lamp and also your signs. (*Seizes lamp*) You won't do it again!

FABIAN: What are you going to do?

JAILOR: Take away the lamp; 'tis the governor's order.

FABIAN (*on his knee*): O, no, no, not now, for mercy's sake!

JAILOR: We know nothing here but obedience. (*Puts out lamp, exists, and locks door*)

FABIAN (*still on his knees*): Heavens! I cannot see, and my letter! (*Goes to window, and then to place where lamp stood*) All is darkness, all is night; the coffin—those mourners; who, who could it be? (*With a cry of despair*) Ah, she—she is dead! (*Falls senseless on the straw. The cannonading begins; noise of musketry. JAILOR appears through trap—gets on staircase*)

JAILOR: They have commenced the attack! Luckily the Bastille is impregnable. (*Goes upstairs, and exits, left door. Reports of cannon at end of scene*)

(*Enter* BRIQUET, *right*)

PIERRE: The cannon! Merciful powers! Why, it's the cannon.

(*Enter* ST. LUCE, *right*)

ST. LUCE (*going to window*): Yes, the artillary of the fortress are firing on the Place St. Antoine; but, by heaven; the Place St. Antoine answers them in their own way!

PIERRE: Heavens! Is it possible?

(*Shouts without*)

ST. LUCE: This is becoming serious! Listen! Those confused cries—that dreadful clamor! (*At window*) And yonder on the ramparts, what a crowd! O, sir, they are no longer soldiers—it is the people!

(*Shouts without, "Victory! Victory!"*)

ST. LUCE: 'Tis impossible; why they'll never take the Bastille like a cockle-shell!

(*Shouts without, "Victory! Victory!" Last discharge of musketry; and the doors are bent in with hatchets; the one at top of stairs falls— several men and soldiers hurry in, some carrying torches, all shouting "Victory!" Listening at door*)

ST. LUCE: They are coming at us!

(*The doors are broken in, and several persons enter the* CHEVALIER'S *apartments; a soldier of the* FRENCH GUARD *is at the head of them*)

ST. LUCE: What is this?

ALL: Liberty! Liberty!

ST. LUCE: How long has it been the fashion to enter the Bastille thus?

SOLDIER: There is no longer a Bastille; tomorrow it will be levelled to the ground; citizen, you are free!

ST. LUCE (*astonished*): Nonsense!

PIERRE (*quickly*): Free! The people fought for us; hurrah for the people!

SOLDIER: Citizens, you are free!

ALL: Liberty! Liberty!

(*All leave room and remain outside*)

ST. LUCE: Certainly, I shall go out, but not this figure! Briquet, quick, my coat and hat! (BRIQUET *enters inner room.* ST. LUCE *takes off dressing gown;* BRIQUET *reenters with necessaries for toilet*)

PIERRE: Here they are, sir. (*Dresses him*)

(*Enter* ANDRE *down staircase, gets amongst crowd, looks about*)

ANDRE: Yes, I'm sure it was in this tower.

SOLDIER: Who are you looking for?

ANDRE: A poor prisoner.

SOLDIER: There is no one else here; there's nothing beneath. Come, let us go.

ALL: Ay, ay.

ANDRE: Nay, stay; I'm sure I'm not mistaken; I am sure beneath our feet a wretched man is perishing, for whom but now I risked my life.

SOLDIER: Look yourself and be satisfied.

ANDRE (*pointing to trap*): This trap, perhaps it may be raised; let us try.

ALL: Yes, yes. (*They all assist with hatchets, etc.*)

ANDRE: Pull it up. (*They raise it*) There, look!

SOLDIER: And do you mean to say there is a living being down there?

ANDRE: Yes, a fellow creature; a good and worthy man. (*Goes down followed by others; one bears a torch*)

ST. LUCE: Now my gloves and my hat. (BRIQUET *gives them*) My sword—ha! I haven't one. Now then, I'll soon to Versailles.

PIERRE: And I to the Park.

(*Both exit up staircase;* BRIQUET *shouting "Hurrah for the people!" At this moment Andre and others break into dungeon below, and, by the torchlight, discover* FABIAN)

ANDRE: Fabian! Fabian! 'Tis I, Andre! (*Raises him*)

FABIAN (*reviving*): Andre! Andre! Are you, too, a prisoner?

ANDRE: No, no; you are free.

FABIAN (*joyfully*): Free! (*Rises, is rushing out, suddenly returns to Andre*) Fool that I am! If they have restored my liberty it is because she is dead—Pauline is dead!

ANDRE: No, no; it was not she—'tis the Marchioness.

FABIAN: And I am free?

ALL: Yes, you are—you are! (*Shouts*) Liberty! Liberty!

(FABIAN *rushes to staircase, then stops suddenly, looks at* ANDRE *and those who surround him; then breaks into a loud fit of laughter; they look sorrowfully at him. 'Tis apparent his reason is gone. At last he falls senseless and exhausted. He is raised by* ANDRE. *Cannon again. The whole back of upper part of scene falls in, and discovers the city, the ramparts, and various groups with torches, etc. Women, citizens, soldiers; red fire, etc.*)

Act IV

An immense gothic apartment in the old Castle of Resadeuc in Bretagne; at the back, a high and vast fireplace; left of fireplace, a large window, opening on a balcony; right of fireplace, a gallery, which is lighted by two painted windows; doors right and left, two each, by side of which hang portraits of the Marquis *and* Marchioness de la Reynerie, *that of the* Marchioness *is right; left, a small table with writing materials, beside it an armchair; right, a sofa; at back, by fireplace, a gothic stool.* Briquet *watching at window,* St. Luce *standing by fireplace;* Aurelia *and* Pauline *seated, warming themselves*

St. Luce (*to* Briquet): Do you see anything strange or suspicious about the chateau?

Pierre: No, sir, I see nothing but the snow and ice. (*Through open window snow is seen falling*) If you will allow me, sir, I'll close the window. (*Shuts it*) Oh, dear! What a precious year is the year 1793!

St. Luce: Go, hasten to the fisherman who promised to let me have his boat to cross to Noman-Mere. Once at sea, either by his own will or by force, he shall take us to England. My sister and my cousin Pauline will not be safe until then. Quick! Quick!

Pierre I'm gone, sir.

(*Exit*)

Aurelia (*rising*): Why take us from this asylum, which the devotion of our tenantry has hitherto rendered so secure.

Pauline (*rising*): My dear friends, why did you expose yourselves for me? Why did you not leave me to die?

Aurelia: Pauline, we may await death in a cell or at the foot of the cross; but to die on a scaffold, exposed to insult from an enraged mob—to die by the hand of the executioner—O, 'tis too dreadful to think of!

Pauline: Those tortures would be but momentary, and my life is one continued agony—you know that my dying mother never forgave poor Fabian, who suddenly disappeared, since when we could never learn if he still lived or had ceased to suffer.

St. Luce: When my sister confided your secret to me, I did all in my power to discover him; I wrote to Bourbon, but none had seen or heard of him; the enraged people disbelieve your marriage, and consider Fabian was sacrificed through your connivance.

AURELIA: Oh, could the late Marchioness see death thus hovering around you, she would call on Fabian to preserve her child; for the proof of the marriage, which is in his possession, would now save her life!

ST. LUCE: Yes, that certificate, signed by the Abbe L'Audrey, who performed the ceremony, would prove her innocence.

(*Enter* BRIQUET)

PIERRE: I could not find the fisherman, sir; but I have brought his brother, who knew all about it.

ST. LUCE (*to* AURELIA): 'Till I have test of this man's fidelity, it would be imprudent to let him see our cousin.

AURELIA (*pointing to door*): We will wait in the library. Come, Pauline.

ST. LUCE: Bring the man in.

(*Exit* BRIQUET)

PAULINE (*looking at portrait*): Mother, mother! Why should we separate again? Here, at the foot of this dear but dreadful image, I would be content to die.

(*Exit with* AURELIA, *right door*)

(*Enter* BRIQUET *with* ANDRE; *he points to* ST. LUCE)

PIERRE: There is the gentleman.

(*Exit at back*)

ST. LUCE (*at table with papers*): Why is it your brother has not come?

ANDRE: He is on a jury at Nantz; I am informed of the business. Bless you, sir, I soon got my hand in again to the old trade; I'll take you quite as safely as my brother.

ST. LUCE: Are you sure of that?

ANDRE: I shall have a steady comrade.

ST. LUCE: Discreet and silent.

ANDRE: Poor fellow, he never speaks to anyone, never remembers anyone! His complaint is all in his brain, and in his heart— so, at least, the doctor says, but his arms are stiff and strong, and the sea breeze does him good. He often spends whole days in the boat, and loves to be rocked by the waves in the clear sunshine; it brings his own country to recollection.

He is very wretched, and I have often heard him mention the names of those who have caused all his sorrows. Then at times he weeps over, and hides again in his bosom, a timeworn discolored paper, which he treasures as a precious relic.

St. Luce (*busy with papers and scarce hearing the latter part of* Andre's *speech*): You will be answerable for this man?

Andre: As for myself, sir.

St. Luce (*putting papers in pocket*): 'Tis well; have you brought him with you?

Andre: Yes sir; he was delighted when he saw me prepare the boat, and I told him we were going for a sail as soon as the tide served.

St. Luce: Where is he?

Andre: Sitting yonder, under the chestnut tree.

St. Luce: Now I'll give you the sum agreed for by your brother.

Andre: I am at your service, sir.

St. Luce: Follow me, then. (*Exit left door, followed by* Andre)

(*Enter* Fabian, *from gallery, right, walks slowly, looking on all sides*)

Fabian: Andre! Andre! The tide is up; we must go. It is still rising—rising! (*Fancying himself surrounded by the waves*) O, save her! Save her! Leave me to perish, I ought to perish—the Abbe L'Audrey! Yes, the poor mulatto will love you—cherish you, even as the mariner does his distant home! (*Sees portrait of Marchioness*) There—there is your mother! (*Supplicating*) Do not curse! No—no, do not curse her! I will go, I will leave her! (*Holds out his arms*) Take her, bind me—send me to a dungeon—to the Bastille, ha! (*A pause*) Hark! The cannon— they are coming! Free! Yes—yes, I am free—free! (Puts hand to head, closes his vest) How I tremble! I am very cold—ha! Some fire, fire!

(*Sits by fire*)

(*Enter* St. Luce *and* Andre, *left door*)

St. Luce: Well, then, now we understand each other, I'll fetch the ladies.

Andre: And I'll bring my comrade. (*Going, sees Fabian*) Ha! There he is, poor fellow! (*Speaks kindly to him*) We are coming on board—don't you hear me? Ha! I see, he has forgotten me again. Come, 'tis I, Andre!

(*Enter* Aurelia *and* Pauline, *right door*)

AURELIA: Courage, Pauline, courage!

(*Enter* ST. LUCE, *right door*)

ST. LUCE: Come, let us be quick.

(*Enter* BRIQUET, *in terror*)

PIERRE: O, sir! O, my lady!

ST. LUCE: What's the matter?

PIERRE: It's all over with us!

ALL: What?

PIERRE: I was keeping a lookout as you desired me, sir, when on a sudden, I saw a number of armed men coming by the Nantz road.

ALL: Nantz!

PIERRE: They are led on by two ill-looking fellows, one of whom I heard say to the rest, pointing to the chateau, "'Tis there she is hid—there you will find the ci-devant Marchioness de la Reynerie!"

ANDRE (*suddenly*): Reynerie!

ST. LUCE: They cannot enter but by force. Come, come—we may yet escape!

(*They are going*)

ANDRE (*aside*): 'Tis she then, the Marchioness, I was about to save!

ST. LUCE (*to* ANDRE): Why do you pause?

ANDRE (*comes down center*) Take back your money—I recall my promise!

ST. LUCE: How say you?

ANDRE (*throws down purse*): I say that for a million of gold I would not guide you!

PAULINE: Heavens! What do you mean?

ANDRE: I mean, lady, I will not aid in the escape of Mademoiselle de la Reynerie—I will not save her whom I have denounced!

ST. LUCE: You wretch!

ANDRE: Justice is for all.

PAULINE: What have I ever done to you?

ANDRE: To me, lady, nothing; had you been my enemy, I could have forgiven you; but you and your family consigned my friend, and benefactor, the best of men, to the foul dungeons of the Bastille!

ST. LUCE: Dare you accuse her?

ANDRE: Yes, and to prove my accusation, I had the jailor's book in my hand, from which I tore a leaf, and there read these words following after my friend's name: "At the request of the family of de Reynerie this man is to be forgotten." I kept that leaf, and have placed it in the hands of the tribunal of Nantz.

ST. LUCE: Wretch! (*Places hand on sword*)

ANDRE: Take my life, but I will not be your guide.

AURELIA (*to* ANDRE): This is a dreadful error; believe me when I swear she is innocent—O, have pity on her.

ANDRE: Pity for her; look at her victim! (*Points to* FABIAN)

ALL: Here!

ANDRE: Yes, there is the martyred victim to the pride of the de la Reynerie.

PAULINE (*with energy, and looking at* FABIAN): Why does he not, then accuse me? Why does he not look at me? I am Pauline de la Reynerie, and before Heaven declare I never injured you.

(FABIAN *raises his head, she recognizes him*)

PAULINE: Fabian!

(*Chord*)

ANDRE: You know him, then?

PAULINE: Fabian!

ANDRE: Yes, look at him; see what the Bastille has done for him.

ALL: The Bastille.

PAULINE (*looking at portrait*): O, mother, mother.

ANDRE: I brought him from there myself; and when I told him he was free, he no longer understood me—his reason had fled.

(FABIAN *comes down, right*)

ALL: Mad.

PAULINE: No, no, I'll not believe it; he will know me. My friend, my husband. Heaven has had pity on us—if but for a day, an hour, it has united us. Heavens! Not one look of joy—not an expression of love in his eyes.

AURELIA: The Bastille, he was in the Bastille.

ANDRE: Yes. When I brought him away they wanted to put him in the madhouse; but then he would but have exchanged his prison; so I took him, and I have shared my crust with him ever since.

PAULINE: Did you do this? (*Takes his hand*) O, may heaven bless you for it. If riches are still left to us, all shall be yours. If I am permitted to live, you shall be our friend, our brother! And if I am to die, my last prayer upon the scaffold shall be for you and for him.

(*Turns to* FABIAN)

ANDRE: What says she? Was Fabian, then—

ST. LUCE: Her husband.

ANDRE: Her husband.

AURELIA: When Fabian was in the Bastille, she too was a prisoner; and now you have destroyed her!

ANDRE: You are not deceiving me? No, no; falsehood has not such accents. Sir, when you are ready we will go.

(*Distant shouts*)

AURELIA (*to* ST. LUCE): Come, come.

ANDRE: Nay, 'tis too late! But fear not, lady, fear not! (*Goes to window*) My brother is amongst them. (*To* AURELIA) Come with me, lady; you are known and respected by all here; they will hear you, and believe you; and you can assist me to repair the wrong I have done.

AURELIA: Yes, yes. Come brother, come.

(*Exit all but* PAULINE *and* FABIAN)

PAULINE (*looking at* FABIAN): Still that dreadful insensibility—still dumb! Heavens! Cannot my tears, my grief, find a way to his heart. (*Falls on her knees before him*)

FABIAN (*looking at her*): Poor Lia! You suffer much! Why do you weep?

PAULINE (*quickly*): You remember Lia! O, then you cannot forget Pauline!

FABIAN: Pauline! Yes—the affianced wife of the Chevalier St. Luce. (*Clock strikes three—he rises*) Three o'clock—she is waiting for me.

PAULINE: Where are you going?

FABIAN: To the Palmtree walk. I will not suffer and die alone. I'll—hush—yes—I'll take her to the Grotto by the sea—we will die together!

PAULINE: Horrible thought.

FABIAN: Hush, the tide is up—at five o'clock.

(*Shouts without*)

PAULINE (*rushes to window*): They are here—they do not believe Andre.

FABIAN (*to himself*): I know the way.

PAULINE: They are coming—they will soon force an entrance. (*Returns to Fabian*) Fabian! One effort to restore his reason—the moment is propitious. You remember the Grotto by the sea?

FABIAN (*to himself*): The tide was rising.

PAULINE: I was resigned, for I thought to die with you, and for you.

FABIAN (*still the same*): The tide was higher.

(*Shouts without*)

PAULINE: They approach. Fabian, do you hear those shouts; today, as in Bourbon, the tempest surrounds us, but much more terrible than the ocean. It is a dreadful mob, thirsting for human blood. (*Now nearer, and she clings to him*) O, Fabian! Save me! Save me!

FABIAN: Now, now, it rises higher, higher.

PAULINE (*looking at him*): Still the same! Heaven, thy will be done. Fabian, when at Bourbon I believed myself dying. I owned I loved you! Fabian, my husband, I love you now. Death is indeed at hand, and my last sigh shall breathe a blessing on your name.

FABIAN (*half recollecting*): Yes, yes; you are Pauline.

PAULINE (*falls on knees*): Merciful heaven, receive my thanks.

(*Noise. Enter* AURELIA *and* ST. LUCE)

AURELIA: They are here, Pauline, they are here.

ST. LUCE: They will see Fabian.

PAULINE (*joyfully*): He has recognized me.

FABIAN (*recognizing* ST. LUCE, *and relapsing immediately*): Still that man forever at her side.

(*Enter* ANDRE, *followed by* CITIZENS, *armed, from balcony and garden*)

PAULINE: Andre! Andre! He has recognized me.

ANDRE (*to all*): Look—brother! See, all, I have not deceived you.

FABIAN (*wildly*): What do these men mean?

AURELIA: Speak, Fabian; tell them Mademoiselle de la Reynerie was ignorant of your captivity in the Bastille.

FABIAN (*in a low voice*): In the Bastille. (*Movement in crowd*)

ANDRE: Tell them she is your wife.

FABIAN (*looking at* MARCHIONESS' s *portrait*): No, no, the Marchioness would kill her; 'tis false, I am not her husband.

(*Murmurs of indignation from mob*)

PAULINE: O, heaven, (*to* FABIAN): you will destroy me.

FABIAN: No, no, hush; I will save you.

PIERRE (*fiercely*): You hear him; he himself accuses her! To Nantz with the aristocrat!

ALL: To Nantz! To Nantz!

ANDRE (*restraining them.—to* PIERRE): Brother, brother! (*A man in gallery, armed with gun, steps forward*)

MAN: We may as well settle it here. (*He fires at* PAULINE, FABIAN *rushes forward, receives the shot, staggers, and falls*)

ANDRE: Wretch, what have you done?

PAULINE (*falls on her knees beside* FABIAN): Murdered—murdered him!

(*People retire confused.* FABIAN *is raised by* CHEVALIER *and* ANDRE; *his reason is returning*)

FABIAN: Pauline, dear Pauline, it is indeed you? (*Trying to recollect*) Ha, ha, again I—

PEOPLE (*rushing forward*): Death to the house of Reynerie.

ANDRE (*in terror*): They will kill her!

FABIAN (*struggling to his feet*): Kill her! (*His reason returns*) Stand off! She is my wife!

ALL: His wife!

ST. LUCE: Yes, his wife.

PIERRE (*advancing*): Show us the proof.

ALL: Ay, ay; the proof.

FABIAN: The proof? 'Tis here. (FABIAN *is supported by* ST. LUCE.; ANDRE *holding* PAULINE *before him;* AURELIA *is on right hand; he opens his vest and produces the marriage certificate, gives it to* PIERRE, *who shows it to people, and they retire up, expressing silent regret. As he opens his vest, blood flows*)

PAULINE (*shuddering*): Ha! There is blood upon his breast! (*Falls on his neck*) They have murdered him!

FABIAN: (*sinking fast*): Pauline, the blow that struck me, was intended for you, and I—I bless heaven, who has granted me to die for—you, for—you! (*dies in their arms*)

Curtain.

A Note About the Author

Ira Aldridge (1807–1867) was a Black actor, playwright and theater manager. Born free in New York, Aldridge had access to a proper education which allowed for exposure to the art of performance through Shakespearian productions put on by the African Theatre. Having developed a love for the stage, he began his acting career in the early 1820s with William Alexander Brown's company, his first professional credits being his roles as Rolla from Richard Sheridan's *Pizarro* and later as Romeo from *Romeo and Juliet*. However, after experiencing several violent protests from white neighbors, Aldridge realized that his ambitions would be limited in America and thus set out for London before his seventeenth birthday and shortly thereafter took to stage in a production of *Othello* making him the first African American to play the character, and possibly the first actor of African descent to do so. In the years that followed, Aldridge traveled throughout the different provinces in England gathering the attention of critics and the admiration of audiences; using his platform to speak directly to theatregoers about the horrors of slavery and racism across the United States, Africa and Europe. He took the roles of Zanga (from *The Revenge*,) King Lear, and at the age of forty adapted the French play, *The Black Doctor* and brought dignity to a role that ended in tragedy for its bi-racial lead. So admired was his talent, that in his lifetime Aldridge continued to break down barriers and became the first African American to manage an English theater. The first in many respects, Ira Aldridge truly was the African Roscius and a symbol of perseverance in the face of racism and discrimination.

A Note from the Publisher

Spanning many genres, from non-fiction essays to literature classics to children's books and lyric poetry, Mint Edition books showcase the master works of our time in a modern new package. The text is freshly typeset, is clean and easy to read, and features a new note about the author in each volume. Many books also include exclusive new introductory material. Every book boasts a striking new cover, which makes it as appropriate for collecting as it is for gift giving. Mint Edition books are only printed when a reader orders them, so natural resources are not wasted. We're proud that our books are never manufactured in excess and exist only in the exact quantity they need to be read and enjoyed. To learn more and view our library, go to minteditionbooks.com

bookfinity & MINT EDITIONS

Enjoy more of your favorite classics with Bookfinity,
a new search and discovery experience for readers.
With Bookfinity, you can discover more vintage
literature for your collection, find your Reader Type,
track books you've read or want to read,
and add reviews to your favorite books.
Visit www.bookfinity.com, and click on
Take the Quiz to get started.

Don't forget to follow us
@bookfinityofficial and @mint_editions